Base Currency Risk

A New Paradigm for Financial Economics

EDWARD CONWAY

First Edition.

Published by Claude Shannon Ltd, 2nd Floor,
145-157 St John Street, London EC1V 4PY

The moral right of the author has been asserted.

Ordering Information:
Quantity sales. Special discounts are available on quantity purchases
by corporations, associations, and others. For details, contact the
publisher at the address above or email sales@claudeshannon.co.uk

Trademarked names may appear in this book. Rather than use a
trademark symbol with every occurrence of a trademarked name,
names are used in an editorial fashion, with no intention of
infringement of the respective owner's trademark.

Any names, characters, places, and incidents either are the product of the author's
imagination or are used fictitiously, and any resemblance to actual persons, living
or dead, events, or locales is entirely coincidental.

The information in this book is distributed on an "as is" basis, without
warranty. Although every precaution has been taken in the preparation of
this work, neither the author nor the publisher shall have any liability
to any person or entity with respect to any loss or damage caused or alleged
to be caused directly or indirectly by the information contained in this book.

To free markets

Base Currency Risk

Edward Conway

Preface

Welcome!

This book is best read straight through one chapter at a time, as material later in the book often uses material presented earlier.

Chapter 2 starts with material that seems so obvious it is safe to skip, but it is actually the crux of the book. So if after reading Chapter 2 you are at all unclear about what RUE is then it may be worth reading it again before continuing.

In terms of mathematics, the focus is on practical application with a minimum of technicalities. This book uses undergraduate linear algebra, probability, statistics, calculus, and stochastic calculus.

Most of this book is original work from 2008-10 and so does not reference possible similar work by others of which I am unaware.

Edward Conway, 2014
bcr@edwardconway.co.uk

Contents

Abstract

Currency risk is all-pervasive in finance and economics, as all financial observations are denominated in risky base currencies. This book presents a new currency independent numeraire based on: (i) no arbitrage, (ii) equal treatment of all assets, and (iii) recognition of base currencies as assets. This generalises existing theory and reinterprets many empirical phenomena as artefacts of arbitrary base currency choice. It is shown that: increased asset volatility coincides with increased correlation between assets; aggregate spot and forward yields are zero; forward prices are biased predictors of future spot prices; and, unaccounted base currency risk solves the Equity Risk Premium Puzzle. A high correlation between the US dollar and US consumption is identified, and this results in US dollar prices approximating a numeraire under which consumption-based asset pricing fails unless log-utility holds. We hypothesise that this correlation is due to widespread pegging of US income and expenditure to US dollar denominated constants.

— 1 —

Introduction

Financial observations are most commonly denominated in fiat[1] base currencies. Fiat currencies are readily accepted mediums of exchange against which we sell our labour, pay taxes and purchase items for investment and consumption. These units of measurement therefore seem natural to us because they are ubiquitous in our daily lives. This has lead to fiat base currencies being commonly employed as units of measurement in financial and economic theory.

The widespread use of an asset as a medium of exchange is a social phenomenon motivated by several factors including: designation by authority, universal acceptability, ease of transfer and carriage, homo-

---

[1]A fiat currency is money declared by a government to be legal tender and demanded in payment of taxes.

geneity, divisibility, an appropriate level of abundance/scarcity, and stability of purchasing power. Whilst popular fiat currencies such as the US dollar are designed to satisfy these criteria, they only do so approximately. In particular, it is widely recognised that inflation and deflation exist and that the purchasing power of fiat currencies varies.

The US dollar price of an apple tells us the ratio at which US dollars and apples can be exchanged for one another. This is the defining feature of prices: they tell us the ratio at which assets can be exchanged for each other. Provided the ratio of exchange remains unchanged it should not matter whether we look at the price of apples denominated in US dollars, or the price of US dollars denominated in apples, or indeed the price of both assets denominated in a third asset such as British pounds, or denominated in some other purely theoretical numeraire.

It is therefore surprising to discover that much existing theory is sensitive to the choice of base currency, even though this choice is arbitrary and does not change the ratios of exchange between assets. For example, a US dollar denominated theory might claim that US dollar cash is risk-free and suitable for investors with highly risk-averse utility. But from the perspective of the same theory denominated in British pounds, US dollar cash is a risky asset and sterling cash is risk-free instead. This definition of risk is therefore dependent on the arbitrary choice of base currency.

The existence of a risk-free rate of return that is earned on an asset with zero risk, denominated in a fiat base currency such as US dollars, is a widely cited assumption. But even if the rate of return on an asset is deterministic (the asset must then be a fixed income asset by definition), the value of the base currency in which the fixed income is denominated remains risky. For example, it may be possible to lock in a 5% return with negligible risk of default, but the currency that this return is denominated in may fall 10% relative to other currencies, or relative to other assets.

The existence of (hyper)inflation and volatility in foreign exchange rates strongly suggests that fiat currencies exhibit risk independently of the risk inherent in other assets. For our purposes, we consider fiat currencies to be standard risky assets, in the same way that equities or commodities are risky assets. We define a new currency independent numeraire to parametrise ratios of exchange, and we call this numeraire the 'Ratio Unit of Exchange', or RUE for short. RUE is motivated by three core principles: (i) no arbitrage, (ii) equal treatment of all assets, and (iii) recognition of base currencies as assets. This framework generalises existing theory and allows us to reinterpret many empirical findings as artefacts of arbitrary base currency choice.

We find that existing theory applies to a RUE denominated world. But when this RUE denominated world is viewed denominated in a risky fiat base currency, the conclusions differ from those obtained by the usual approach of applying theory directly to fiat currency denominated variables. These differences result in an improved fit between theory and reality.

The RUE framework automatically results in fiat base currency denominated price dynamics consistent with the empirically observed phenomena that the volatilities of different assets often move together, and that increased asset volatility coincides with increased correlation between assets.

A consumption-based asset pricing model is introduced and spot and forward yields on the Market portfolio are shown to be identically zero. Forward foreign exchange rates are shown to be biased predictors of spot foreign exchange rates, and this result applies generally to the forward prices of all assets.

CAPM is then derived as a special case of the pricing model, where a function of consumption is approximated linearly by the Market portfolio. However, we later discover an empirically high correlation between US dollar cash and US consumption that suggests this function would be better approximated linearly by US dollar cash, which in turn suggests that US dollar cash approximates systematic risk under CAPM. This is in stark contrast to the conventional view that US dollar cash is risk free.

We then identify a numeraire under which utility is risk-neutral. It is shown that log-utility either applies under all numeraires or nowhere at all. We also find that if log-utility does not hold then consumption-based asset pricing fails under base currencies perfectly correlated with consumption.

Finally, we apply the RUE framework to the US Equity Risk Premium Puzzle and discover it can be explained by unaccounted base currency risk. We discover a high empirical correlation between RUE denominated US consumption and the RUE price of the US dollar that suggests US dollars are an approximation to a numeraire under which consumption-based asset pricing fails unless log-utility holds. We hypothesise that this correlation is due to widespread pegging of US income and expenditure to US dollar denominated constants.

— 2 —

Ratio Unit of Exchange (RUE)

If the barter ratio of exchange for oranges rises from two to three apples per orange, we don't know whether: (a) oranges have become more valuable, (b) apples have become less valuable, (c) oranges have become more valuable and apples have become less valuable, (d) oranges have become less valuable but apples have become less valuable to a greater extent, or (e) apples have become more valuable but oranges have become more valuable to a greater extent.

When existing theories consider price movements denominated in a base currency, the base currency asset is substituted for apples and option (a) is generally assumed. The equally valid possibilities (b), (c), (d) and (e) are implicitly assumed away. Here we provide a simple framework that can be used to restore these possibilities by allowing the prices of all assets to vary, without exception.

2.1   The RUE Framework

The RUE framework is a very general construction based on three core principles: (i) no arbitrage, (ii) equal treatment of all assets, and (iii) recognition of base currencies as assets.

We assume a market of $N + 1 \geq 2$ homogeneous and perfectly divisible tradable assets in which trading takes place continuously and short selling is allowed. Consistent with principle (iii), we regard base currencies as tradable assets in their own right.

Consistent with principle (ii) we assume that all tradable assets are exchangeable for other assets at some time-varying positive ratio of exchange. Let $E_{ij}(t) > 0$ be the amount of asset j that is exchangeable for one unit of asset i at time $t \in [0, \infty)$.

If there is no instantaneous arbitrage at time t then for all $i, j \in \{0, 1, \ldots, N\}$

$$E_{ij}(t) = 1/E_{ji}(t). \tag{2.1}$$

In addition, for all $i, j, k \in \{0, 1, \ldots, N\}$ we require for absence of arbitrage that

$$E_{ij}(t) = E_{ik}(t)E_{kj}(t). \tag{2.2}$$

Consistent with principle (i), we assume that instantaneous arbitrage opportunities at any time t are sufficiently obvious to be fully exploited, so equations (2.1) and (2.2) hold.

We can then conveniently parametrise this arrangement, consistent with principle (ii), by assigning a price process, $P_i(t) > 0$, to each asset $i \in \{0, 1, \ldots, N\}$ such that $E_{ij}(t) = P_i(t)/P_j(t)$ for all $i, j \in \{0, 1, \ldots, N\}$. We call the units these prices are measured in the 'Ratio Unit of Exchange', or RUE for short.

When we say an apple is worth $1, we mean that apples and US dollars are exchangeable at a rate of $1 per apple. Usually prices involve the ratio of two assets, because they are used to gauge the value of assets *relative* to one another. A list of three US dollar stock prices relates the relative values of four assets: the three stocks, plus US dollars. In contrast, the RUE framework assigns each single asset an individual RUE price, so the number of RUE prices always equals the number of assets. Each asset has its own RUE price that applies to it alone.

For every asset i there is a corresponding RUE price process, $P_i(t)$, and the ratios of these price processes tell us the ratios of exchange between assets. For example, if $P_\$(t)$ is the RUE price process of one US dollar then the US dollar price of asset i is given by $P_i(t)/P_\$(t)$. Similarly, if $P_£(t)$ is the RUE price process of one British pound then the sterling price of asset i is given by $P_i(t)/P_£(t)$. The GBP/USD foreign exchange rate[1] is then given by $P_£(t)/P_\$(t)$.

If we know the RUE price process $P_j(t)$ of asset j we can calculate the corresponding RUE price process of each asset $i \in \{0, 1, \ldots, N\}$ as follows:

$$P_i(t) := P_j(t)E_{ij}(t). \tag{2.3}$$

The RUE price processes, $P_i(t)$ for $i \in \{0, 1, \ldots, N\}$, are therefore unique up to a single time-varying factor, namely, the RUE price process of asset j.

In keeping with principle (ii), we assume that the RUE price processes $P_i(t)$ obey dynamics of an identical general form for every

---

[1]The number of US dollars exchangeable for one British pound.

asset $i \in \{0, 1, \ldots, N\}$. This assumption means that risk in ratios of exchange is attributable to RUE asset price dynamics via a process of statistical estimation that treats all assets equally.

For the avoidance of doubt, we can choose any general form we please for RUE price process dynamics as long as we use the same general form for each asset. When we come to statistically estimate the parameters of this general form we will find that different assets have different parameter values and behave differently as a result. The important point is that we have let the process of statistical estimation using empirical data tell us about these differences without imposing them as assumptions. Each asset is subject to equal treatment in this process of parameter estimation, and any eventual differences in asset behaviour arise from unbiased analysis of empirical data.

In summary, the RUE framework proposes that:

1. Every asset $i \in \{0, 1, \ldots, N\}$ is assigned a price process $P_i(t) > 0$.

2. Each price process $P_i(t)$ has dynamics of an identical general form.

3. The ratios of exchange between assets are given by the ratios of the price processes, so $E_{ij}(t) = P_i(t)/P_j(t)$ for all $i, j \in \{0, 1, \ldots, N\}$.

The RUE numeraire is therefore a transformation of commonly observed market prices that is equally consistent with observed market behaviour (ratios of exchange) as the raw market prices, but exhibits symmetry in the sense that all assets are treated equally, whether they are fiat currencies or not. This symmetrical parametrisation of relative value and risk, where each asset's RUE price dynamics describe the risk attributable to that asset, avoids the usual practice of arbitrarily specifying a base currency asset.

2.2   Comparison with Base Currencies

The usual base currency approach proposes that:

1. Every asset $i \in \{0, 1, \ldots, N\}$ is assigned a price process $P_i(t) > 0$.

2. The price process of the base currency asset $b \in \{0, 1, \ldots, N\}$ is identically one, $P_b(t) \equiv 1$.

3. The ratios of exchange between assets are given by the ratios of the price processes, so $E_{ij}(t) = P_i(t)/P_j(t)$ for all $i, j \in \{0, 1, \ldots, N\}$.

Prices denominated in a base currency coincide with RUE prices if and only if the RUE price process of the base currency asset is identically one. Using an asset as a base currency is therefore consistent with no risk inherent to that asset under RUE, our symmetric parametrisation of risk. For example, using US dollar prices is equivalent to using RUE prices where we have set the RUE price process of US dollars identically equal to one. Using US dollars as a base currency is therefore consistent with no risk attributable to the US dollar asset under RUE. There is therefore an asymmetry in the treatment of the base currency asset versus all other assets under the usual base currency approach.

We require the RUE framework because base currencies are assets themselves, subject to the pressures of supply and demand, and exhibiting risk. For example, if $P_\$$ is the RUE price of US dollars, equal to the number of RUE per one US dollar, or in exchange rate notation, USD/RUE, then the process $P_\$(t) > 0$ for $t \in [0, \infty)$ captures all the risk attributable to one US dollar. A bout of hyperinflation in US dollar denominated prices is then easily explained by a rapid decline in the value of $P_\$$ relative to the RUE prices of all other assets, and so is attributable to the behaviour of the US dollar asset[2]. Under the usual base currency approach, using the US dollar asset as a base currency, the RUE price process of the US dollar asset is identically one. So hyperinflation is attributable to a simultaneous change in the behaviour of all assets except the US dollar asset. This attribution of events seems unnecessarily complex and relatively unlikely to reflect reality.

Naturally, it is entirely possible that the RUE price of a popular base currency, such as US dollars, is constant and the RUE numeraire is superfluous. However, this is unlikely due to three reasons. Firstly, the existence of inflation and hyperinflation provide strong empirical evidence that prices often move in ways that are most easily explained by changes in the RUE price of the base currency concerned. Secondly, volatility in foreign exchange rates (e.g. $P_\pounds/P_\$$) tells us that the relative values of different fiat currency assets varies considerably, and so if there does exist an unusual fiat currency with constant RUE price, other fiat currencies cannot share this unique property. Finally, there are many other equally plausible candidates

---

[2]The fact that some assets inflate more than others can be explained by RUE asset prices having varying correlations with the RUE price of the base currency asset.

that might be considered to have constant RUE price: gold, silver, oil, water, apples, EUR, CNY, human life, energy, information and units of utility, to name a few.

RUE is a generalisation of the usual base currency approach. If it transpires that the RUE price process of any asset is constant with zero drift then this asset is a substitute for RUE, and the RUE framework is equivalent to the usual base currency approach as long as we use the constant RUE price asset as our base currency. The beauty of the RUE framework is that we do not have to specify in advance what this base currency asset is.

The choice of base currency is crucially important for theories of finance that rely on rationalising the behaviour of market participants in response to risk. For example, a market participant using US dollars as a base currency might be expected to demand a risk-premium for abandoning the relative safety of US dollar cash and investing in a sterling cash account, whereas a market participant using British pounds as a base currency might be expected to demand a risk-premium for abandoning the relative safety of sterling cash and investing in a US dollar cash account. If we chose the Market portfolio as our base currency we could equally argue that investors require a risk-premium for abandoning the relative safety of the Market portfolio and investing in cash.

Perspectives on risk, and the rational behaviour they motivate, are shaped by choice of base currency. The fact that base currency choice is currently largely arbitrary bodes ill for the ability of any economic or financial theory based on risk preferences to fit empirical data. The usual base currency approach suffers from the arbitrary nature of the choice of base currency asset $b \in \{0, 1, \ldots, N\}$ which is effectively an arbitrarily specified risk-free asset, thus destroying any objectivity in the analysis of relative risk.

We therefore require a special non-arbitrary numeraire for financial and economic analysis, to avoid the arbitrary influence of base currency choice. For a consistent definition of risk we must restrict ourselves to a set of numeraires that agree on the relative risks of different assets. The major problem here is that we do not necessarily know in advance what this numeraire is. The RUE framework is a way of working under a general numeraire. This allows us to generalise financial theories so that they apply to the non-arbitrary set of numeraires in which they apply, if such a set exists, without us needing to identify these numeraires in advance.

We later introduce a set of investable basis assets and identify a theoretical asset with zero volatility and drift denominated in RUE. This means that the RUE framework is equivalent to the usual base currency approach using this constant RUE price asset as the base currency asset. This can be thought of as the usual base currency approach with non-arbitrary base currency choice.

From a practical perspective, the primary disadvantage of RUE prices is that they are not directly observable and need to be estimated statistically. This process of statistical estimation is dependent on the empirical data used and the general form of the dynamics assumed for RUE price processes. We later provide two methods of estimating RUE prices from empirical price data assuming geometric Brownian RUE price dynamics.

Under the RUE framework, no distinction is made between fiat currencies and other assets. So even in a world with only one fiat currency, other non-fiat currency assets can still be used as base currencies. Arguments in favour of the RUE framework therefore survive in a world with only one fiat currency as long as it is still equally possible to look at the world denominated in other assets.

Even in a world where barter is not possible in practise, we can still trade via the fiat currency at the theoretical no-arbitrage barter ratio of exchange. To arrive at the usual base currency approach we would need to argue that none of the movement in fiat currency denominated prices is attributable to the fiat currency asset. This is difficult to argue statistically given inflation and deflation, which are widely recognised as resulting from changes in the purchasing power of the fiat base currency.

2.3   Investable Basis

To provide a simple framework in which to model market behaviour under RUE, we assume a basis of tradable assets. Assume that under RUE there are $N + 1$ independent assets. We denote the total value of each basis asset i denominated in RUE at time t by $A_i(t) > 0$ for $i \in \{0, 1, \ldots, N\}$ and $t \in [0, \infty)$.

The basis spans the entire Market. This means that any asset can be instantaneously represented by a linear combination of basis assets. The total value of the Market, $M(t) > 0$ for $t \in [0, \infty)$, is defined to be the total value in RUE of all assets that have value.

Therefore

$$M(t) := \sum_{i=0}^{N} A_i(t). \tag{2.4}$$

The Market includes all fiat currencies, equities, bonds, commodities, real estate assets and economic factors of production that are available in return for other assets. Among other things, this includes human labour, entrepreneurialism, and black market assets. Anything with a ratio of exchange is included.

The basis is orthogonal, with each basis asset uncorrelated to every other. This can be thought of as the result of a principal components decomposition of all RUE denominated assets in the Market into orthogonal principal components.

We assume a probability space $(\Omega, \mathcal{F}, \mathbb{P})$, where Ω represents the state-space, and $\mathbb{P}$ is the probability measure. The filtration $\mathcal{F}_s :=$ $\{\mathcal{F} : s \in [0, t]\}$ represents all the information available at time s from the σ-algebra representing all measurable events, $\mathcal{F}$.

The risky basis assets are driven by a collection of N independent Brownian motions $\{W_1(t), \ldots, W_N(t) : t \in [0, \infty)\}$. We assume the dynamics of basis asset i are given by the following geometric

Brownian motion:

$$\frac{dA_i(t)}{A_i(t)} \; = \; \mu_i(\mathcal{F}_t)dt + \sigma_i(\mathcal{F}_t)dW_i(t) \tag{2.5}$$

for all $i \in \{1, 2, \ldots, N\}$ and $t \in [0, \infty)$, with

$$\langle dW_i, dW_j \rangle = \delta_{ij}dt \tag{2.6}$$

for all $i, j \in \{1, 2, \ldots, N\}$, where $\langle a, b \rangle$ denotes the cross-quadratic variation of a and b, and δ_{ij} is the Kronecker delta equal to one if $i = j$ and zero otherwise. The drift of asset i, $\mu_i(\mathcal{F}_t)$, and volatility of asset i, $\sigma_i(\mathcal{F}_t) > 0$, are adapted to the filtration, $\mathcal{F}_t$, equivalent to all information known at time t.

In order to be able to import existing theory into the RUE framework we allow for a RUE denominated risk-free asset A_0 corresponding to $i = 0$. This asset follows RUE price dynamics of the same general form as all the other assets, except with volatility set to zero, $\sigma_0 \equiv 0$. For readers uncomfortable with this assumption on the grounds that we do not know in advance if such a risk-free basis asset exists denominated in RUE, it is possible to think of this asset as an approximation to the least risky asset that could be obtained by forming a minimum volatility portfolio from all the basis assets available.

For each basis asset, $i \in \{0, 1, \ldots, N\}$, we denote the total quantity of the asset by $Q_i(t) > 0$ and the RUE price of the asset by $P_i(t) > 0$, where $A_i(t) = P_i(t)Q_i(t)$ for $t \in [0, \infty)$. In this book, the quantities of basis assets are assumed constant. So for all assets $i \in \{0, 1, \ldots, N\}$, $dA_i = Q_i dP_i$ and so

$$\frac{dA_i}{A_i} \equiv \frac{dP_i}{P_i}. \tag{2.7}$$

This may appear an unrealistic assumption, however, recall that our basis spans all investable assets. This means that, with the exception of new investable assets being unexpectedly discovered, or created out of something with zero value, changes in quantities are largely illusory. If A and B are basis assets, the combination of A and B into a new compound asset C does not change the quantities of the basis assets A and B, only their cosmetic appearance.

Due to assuming the existence of the risk-free asset A_0, only N of our $N + 1$ basis assets are risky. This can be compared to the situation under the usual base currency approach where only N of the $N + 1$ assets are risky due to the base currency asset being assumed risk-free. The RUE framework with a risk-free basis asset has the same dimensionality of Market risk as the usual base currency approach. The crucial distinction is that A_0 is a generalised risk-free basis asset and we do not pre-specify its composition in terms of real-world assets, whereas the risk-free asset under the usual base currency approach is an arbitrarily selected real-world asset.

Recall that RUE prices are a symmetrical parametrisation of risk and return in the observable ratios of exchange between assets. The risk-free asset A_0 is instantaneously risk-free denominated in RUE, but will appear risky denominated in any base currency asset (except itself) due to the risk in the RUE price of the base currency. For example, the US dollar denominated price of the risk-free asset $A_0/P_\$$ is risky due to the volatility of the US dollar asset. We speculate that A_0 is likely to resemble a well-diversified global portfolio of assets.

2.4   Net Income Yields

Under the usual base currency approach it is clear that the value of the base currency asset denominated in the base currency is identically one, $P_b(t)/P_b(t) \equiv 1$. This means that the base currency asset has no volatility or drift denominated in itself. So the spot yield (interest rate) denominated in this base currency is constrained by no-arbitrage arguments to be identically zero unless we argue that either the base currency asset is not tradable and should not be technically recognised as a tradable asset, or posit the existence of some other mechanism resulting in non-zero spot yields. The former line of reasoning contradicts the fact that it is the ratios of exchange with the base currency asset that define our base currency denominated prices in the first place.

Under the RUE framework we treat each asset equally, and so do not award fiat currency assets special features beyond those enjoyed by all other assets. This leaves us with no choice in recognising that in the absence of some other mechanism applying to all assets equally, base currency spot yields are constrained to be identically zero. We now introduce a mechanism called Net Income Yields. These are consistent with economic behaviour, and allow for non-zero interest rates and spot yields. Equal treatment of all assets necessitates a clear distinction between prices, that tell us about ratios of exchange, and other mechanisms that result in non-zero spot or forward yields.

We define Net Income Yields to be returns that accrue to holders of an asset as a benefit or cost attached to asset ownership, separately and in addition to returns resulting from changes in ratios of exchange.

All assets have the ability to earn economic rent or incur a cost of carry for their holder. Net Income Yields are income streams (transfers of wealth) that accrue to the holders of assets, but do not accrue directly to the ratio of exchange between assets.

For example, bond coupons are a Net Income Yield accruing to bond holders, dividend yields are a Net Income Yield accruing to stock holders, and the cost of carry for copper is a Net Income Yield accruing to holders of physical copper. In particular, interest rates are a Net Income Yield accruing to holders of fiat currency assets.

Consistent with the principle of equal treatment of all assets, we define a Net Income Yield process $y_i(t) \in \mathbb{R}$ for each basis asset i for $i \in \{0, 1, \ldots, N\}$ such that the RUE denominated income accruing to the holder of basis asset i over time interval dt as a result of Net Income Yield is $y_i(t)A_i(t)dt$. So a portfolio P holding basis asset i and reinvesting Net Income Yield into basis asset i grows according to $dP/P = (\mu_i + y_i)dt + \sigma_i dW_i$. Each $y_i(t)$ is free to vary stochastically, is instantaneously risk-free, and is adapted to the filtration $\mathcal{F}_t$.

Being short an asset earns negative the Net Income Yield. The reason for this is that an asset must be borrowed before it can be sold short. If an asset pays a positive Net Income Yield the holder lending the asset needs to be compensated by the borrower for the Net Income Yield they forgo during the period the asset is lent. Similarly, if the Net Income Yield to the asset holder is negative the borrower needs to receive negative the Net Income Yield to compensate them for the cost of carrying the asset. This is consistent with market behaviour. Someone who is short cash must pay interest (Net Income Yield) rather than earning it, likewise, someone who is short stock must pay the dividends (Net Income Yield) earned by the stock to the stock lender.

Consider a RUE denominated portfolio with value P holding US dollars and reinvesting Net Income Yield into the US dollar asset. Let the RUE price of one US dollar be given by $P_\$$ with

$$dP_\$/P_\$ \;=\; \mu_\$ dt + \sigma_\$ dW_\$^*, \tag{2.8}$$

where $\mu_\$$ is the drift and $\sigma_\$$ is the volatility of $P_\$$, and $W_\$^*$ is the Brownian motion driving US dollar RUE price risk. If the Net Income Yield for the US dollar asset is $y_\$$ then the RUE price dynamics of the portfolio P are given by

$$dP/P \;=\; (\mu_\$ + y_\$)dt + \sigma_\$ dW_\$^*. \qquad (2.9)$$

The US dollar price of the portfolio is given by $P/P_\$$ so the US dollar denominated dynamics for a portfolio of US dollars are given via Itô by

$$d[P/P_\$]/[P/P_\$] \;=\; y_\$ dt. \qquad (2.10)$$

This shows that the spot rate on a portfolio of US dollars, denominated in the US dollar asset, is equal to the Net Income Yield for the US dollar asset. This is because one US dollar is always worth one US dollar, so the price of US dollars denominated in US dollars is constant with zero drift. A US dollar cash account will therefore earn zero spot rate due to movements in the RUE price of US dollars, and relies on wealth to flow into the account if spot rates are to be positive as empirically observed.

Given that US dollars are not given special treatment under the

RUE framework, a corresponding result holds for all other assets. The spot rate on any portfolio, denominated in the assets held in that portfolio, equals the Net Income Yield of that portfolio. For example, the spot dividend rate on a portfolio of equities is equal to the Net Income Yield of that portfolio of equities.

Recall that the RUE denominated value of the Market portfolio, denoted M, and representing the total value of all assets, is given by

$$M \; = \; \sum_{i=0}^{N} A_i \tag{2.11}$$

which tells us that

$$dM \; = \; \sum_{i=0}^{N} [A_i \mu_i dt + A_i \sigma_i dW_i] . \tag{2.12}$$

Now consider the value of a portfolio, P, that owns the Market portfolio. We know by definition that $M \equiv P$ because the Market is the value of all assets, so $dM \equiv dP$. But ownership confers the ability of the holder to earn Net Income Yield, so the instantaneous dynamics for the value of the portfolio are given by

$$dP = \sum_{i=0}^{N} [A_i(\mu_i + y_i)dt + \sigma_i dW_i] = dM. \qquad (2.13)$$

It follows from equations (2.12) and (2.13) that the aggregate Net Income Yield must be identically zero. The Net Income Yield of the Market portfolio must be zero because Net Income Yields are transfers of wealth, and the Market portfolio already holds all assets.

$$\sum_{i=0}^{N} A_i y_i \equiv 0. \qquad (2.14)$$

Another way of stating this result is to say that the Net Income Yield of the Market portfolio is identically zero, $y_M \equiv 0$. This tells us that any portfolio with a non-zero Net Income Yield cannot be the Market portfolio. For example, the S&P 500 earns a positive Net Income Yield due to dividends so cannot be the Market portfolio.

2.5   Risk-Free Returns

We denote the instantaneous risk-free rate of return under RUE by $r \in \mathbb{R}$ and define a risk-free asset A_0 under RUE with dynamics

$$\frac{dA_0(t)}{A_0(t)} = \mu_0(\mathcal{F}_t)dt. \qquad (2.15)$$

The instantaneous risk-free rate, $r = \mu_0 + y_0$, is the instantaneous rate of return on a portfolio holding the risk-free asset, is free to vary stochastically, and is adapted to the filtration $\mathcal{F}_t$. The risk-free rate under RUE is a combination of the RUE price drift μ_0 and the Net Income Yield y_0 enjoyed by holders of the risk-free asset A_0.

Existing theory assumes that risk-free rates of return are positive, due to investors' ability to hoard physical cash and earn a zero return. Under RUE, there is no such constraint. Hoarding physical cash will result in the return of the risky fiat currency asset concerned, denominated in RUE. There is therefore no refuge from risk with the exception of the risk-free asset, A_0. There is no constraint that the risk-free rate of return, r, will be greater or equal to zero.

If there existed two risk-free assets with prices $A > 0$ and $B > 0$ under RUE and risk-free rates $r_A = \mu_A + y_A$ and $r_B = \mu_B + y_B$

respectively, with $r_A > r_B$, an arbitrageur could make unlimited risk-free profit under RUE by going long the higher yielding risk-free asset, and short the lower yielding one. In practical terms, this arbitrage could be conducted using the ratio of exchange, $E_{AB} = A/B$, to simultaneously build up short exposure in B, and long exposure in A. We assume that such an arbitrage is not possible, so $r_A \equiv r_B$. Therefore $r = \mu_0 + y_0$ is instantaneously unique.

In practical terms, to invest in A_0 it would first be necessary to estimate RUE price volatilities. Investing to minimise portfolio volatility under RUE would then approximate an investment in the risk-free asset A_0. Speculating, we imagine that A_0 would resemble a well-diversified global portfolio that would ironically appear risky when denominated in US dollars, due to US dollar risk.

Recall that if an asset exists with constant RUE price and zero drift then RUE prices coincide with prices under the usual base currency approach using this asset as a base currency. So if $\mu_0 = 0$ then the asset A_0 is a substitute for RUE.

Theoretically, it is possible to construct a hypothetical structured product holding the asset A_0 as collateral and issuing risk-free RUE notes worth 1 RUE each and paying out a Net Income Yield of $r = \mu_0 + y_0$. The RUE price of these notes will then have zero drift due to the uniqueness of r. The RUE numeraire is therefore equivalent to the usual base currency approach using one of these notes as the base currency asset, and 1 RUE is equivalent to the value of one of these notes.

$$- 3 -$$

Implications for Price Dynamics

Using the RUE framework, we now consider how prices denominated in a base currency asset would appear to behave due to the risky nature of the base currency under RUE. We find that changes in base currency volatility drive simultaneous changes in base currency denominated volatilities and correlations.

3.1   Asset Volatilities

For simplicity, we restrict our attention here to just three RUE denominated assets, A, B, and C. Let $C(t) > 0$ be the price of a fiat base currency such as US dollars, and let $A(t) > 0$ and $B(t) > 0$ represent the prices of two correlated assets. All three assets follow geometric Brownian motion for which we assume that

$$dA/A \;=\; \mu_A dt + \sigma_A dW_A, \qquad (3.1)$$

$$dB/B \;=\; \mu_B dt + \sigma_B dW_B, \qquad (3.2)$$

$$dC/C \;=\; \mu_C dt + \sigma_C dW_C, \qquad (3.3)$$

$$\langle dW_A, dW_B \rangle \;=\; \rho_{AB} dt, \qquad (3.4)$$

$$\langle dW_A, dW_C \rangle \;=\; 0, \qquad (3.5)$$

$$\langle dW_B, dW_C \rangle \;=\; 0, \qquad (3.6)$$

with μ_A, μ_B, μ_C constant, $\sigma_A(t), \sigma_B(t), \sigma_C(t) > 0$, and $-1 < \rho_{AB}(t) < +1$.

Denote the ratio of exchange between asset A and asset C by $E_{AC} = A/C$, then the price of asset A denominated in fiat base currency C is E_{AC}.

Via Itô we obtain the dynamics

$$dE_{AC}/E_{AC} \;=\; (\mu_A - \mu_C + \sigma_C^2)dt + \qquad (3.7)$$

$$\sigma_A dW_A - \sigma_C dW_C,$$

$$d\log E_{AC} \;=\; \left(\mu_A - \mu_C + \frac{1}{2}\sigma_C^2 - \frac{1}{2}\sigma_A^2\right)dt + \qquad (3.8)$$

$$\sigma_A dW_A - \sigma_C dW_C.$$

Base currency volatility therefore contributes simultaneously to both the volatility and drift of base currency denominated returns.

It follows that when we calculate the variance of the returns of asset A denominated in base currency C, we are really calculating the variance of the returns of E_{AC} as follows:

$$\mathrm{VAR}(d\log E_{AC}) = \left\langle \frac{dE_{AC}}{E_{AC}} \right\rangle = (\sigma_A^2 + \sigma_C^2)dt, \qquad (3.9)$$

where $\langle a \rangle$ denotes the quadratic variation of process a.

The volatility of an asset denominated in a fiat base currency is thus an increasing function of the fiat currency volatility[1]. So all other things equal, an increase in base currency volatility under RUE will simultaneously increase the variances of asset prices denominated in that base currency.

The commonly accepted explanation for asset variances moving together is that prices are driven by exposure to common risk factors. To this explanation we add base currency risk as an additional contributor, although changes in base currency volatility also cause the variances of otherwise uncorrelated assets to move together.

While it is possible to think of base currency risk as just another risk-factor, base currency risk is a risk imposed on prices due to our decision to use a particular base currency. This risk is therefore a matter of personal perspective rather than an objective influence on underlying economic reality.

---

[1]Assuming here the simple case of no correlation between the asset and the fiat base currency. However, even with non-zero correlation a sufficiently large increase in base currency volatility will always increase the volatility of an asset denominated in that base currency.

3.2   Asset Correlations

When we calculate the covariance between the returns of assets A and B, both denominated in fiat base currency C, we are really calculating the covariance between the returns of E_{AC} and E_{BC} as follows:

$$\mathbb{COV}(d \log E_{AC}, d \log E_{BC}) = \left\langle \frac{dE_{AC}}{E_{AC}}, \frac{dE_{BC}}{E_{BC}} \right\rangle \quad (3.10)$$

$$= (\rho_{AB}\sigma_A\sigma_B + \sigma_C^2)dt.$$

So the covariance between asset returns denominated in a fiat base currency is a strictly increasing function of the fiat currency volatility[2].

The correlation between the returns of assets A and B when viewed denominated in the fiat currency C is given by

$$\text{Corr}(d \log E_{AC}, d \log E_{BC}) = \frac{\sigma_A\sigma_B\rho_{AB} + \sigma_C^2}{\sqrt{(\sigma_A^2 + \sigma_C^2)(\sigma_B^2 + \sigma_C^2)}}. \quad (3.11)$$

---

[2]A sufficiently large increase in base currency volatility will increase asset return covariances irrespective of asset return correlations with the base currency (that are here assumed zero).

It can be seen that even if the actual correlation between A and B is zero, base currency volatility will result in them appearing to have a positive correlation.

If $\sigma_A = \sigma_B$ then correlation is a strictly increasing function of base currency volatility as follows:

$$\frac{\partial}{\partial \sigma_C} \text{Corr}(d \log E_{AC}, d \log E_{BC}) \tag{3.12}$$

$$= \frac{2 \sigma_C \sigma_A^2}{(\sigma_A^2 + \sigma_C^2)^2}(1 - \rho_{AB})$$

$$> 0.$$

Define

$$\sigma_{AB}^2 := \sigma_A^2 + \sigma_B^2 - 2\rho_{AB}\sigma_A\sigma_B, \tag{3.13}$$

then for $\sigma_A \neq \sigma_B$ we see that correlation is still an increasing function of base currency volatility if

$$\text{sign}\left[\frac{\partial}{\partial \sigma_C} \text{Corr}(d \log E_{AC}, d \log E_{BC})\right] \tag{3.14}$$

$$= \text{sign}\left(\sigma_C^2 \sigma_{AB}^2 + [2\sigma_A\sigma_B - \rho_{AB}(\sigma_A^2 + \sigma_B^2)]\sigma_A\sigma_B\right)$$

$$> 0.$$

Or equivalently,

$$\frac{\sigma_C^2 \sigma_{AB}^2 + 2\sigma_A^2 \sigma_B^2}{(\sigma_A^2 + \sigma_B^2)\sigma_A \sigma_B} > \rho_{AB}. \tag{3.15}$$

This condition is always satisfied when $\rho_{AB} \leq 0$. It also tends to be satisfied unless the return volatilities of A and B are very different, or unless the correlation between them is close to perfect. Importantly, it holds irrespective of correlation when σ_C is sufficiently large.

Therefore, all other things equal, an increase in base currency volatility under RUE will tend to simultaneously increase both the variances of, and the correlations[3] between, assets denominated in that base currency.

Andersen, Bollerslev, Diebold, and Ebens [1] studied the realised volatility and correlation of thirty US stocks. They found strong evidence that the variances of different stocks tend to move together, and that correlations tend to be higher when volatilities are higher. They wrote that "there is a systematic tendency for the variances to move together, and for the correlations among the different stocks to be high/low when the variances for the underlying stocks are

---

[3]With a few exceptions when equation (3.15) is not satisfied. However, for a sufficiently large increase in base currency volatility this condition is always satisfied.

high/low, and when the correlations among the other stocks are also high/low."

While this can be partially explained by changes in the volatility of risk factors, an additional explanation for these findings (and similar behaviour in the volatilities and correlations of different asset classes) is variation in base currency volatility. Changes in base currency volatility drive simultaneous changes in asset volatilities, and asset correlations. When base currency volatility is high, the volatility of individual assets, and the correlation between assets (with some exceptions when equation (3.15) is not satisfied), will both tend to be high, and vice-versa.

— 4 —

Consumption-Based Asset Pricing

To price assets we now introduce a consumption-based model whereby current prices are assumed to be the result of optimal trading strategies maximising expected aggregate utility. Forward yields are then shown to be the result of expected future Net Income Yields. As a consequence of this, instantaneous forward yields on the Market portfolio are identically zero.

The price of base currency zero coupon bonds is then derived. From this, the standard formula for forward foreign exchange rates is obtained and forward foreign exchange rates are shown to be biased predictors of spot foreign exchange rates.

4.1 Consumption-Based Pricing Equation

The key idea behind this pricing model is that market participants engage in trading strategies to maximise the expected aggregate utility of their consumption over time. This kind of approach is well explained in Cochrane's book 'Asset Pricing' [2].

We assume the existence of a single representative 'stand-in' household with utility function $u : \mathbb{R} \to \mathbb{R}$. In continuous time, the rate that utility is obtained from RUE denominated consumption at rate c_v is $u(c_v)$. The expected aggregate utility of consumption at time t is then

$$U_t := \mathbb{E}\left[\left.\int_t^\infty \beta(t,v)u(c_v)dv \right| \mathcal{F}_t\right], \qquad (4.1)$$

where $\beta(t,v) \in \mathbb{R}$ for $t,v \in [0,\infty)$ with $v \geq t$ and $\beta(t,t) \equiv 1$ is the subjective discount factor applied to discount utility from consumption at time v and is known at time t with $\beta(t,v) \in \mathcal{F}_t$. This subjective discount factor represents impatience.

Market participants act to maximise U_t at time t. If e_t is an initial rate of RUE denominated consumption at time t then $e_t + P_\star(t)\xi_t$ is also a possible rate of consumption at time t as a result of selling units of a general asset $P_\star$ with RUE price $P_\star(t)$ at a rate ξ_t. If

$y_\star(v)$ is the Net Income Yield accruing to holders of asset $P_\star$ then the total rate at which Net Income Yield revenue flows into the portfolio at time v due to the trading strategy defined by $\xi_s \in \mathbb{R}$ for $s \in [t, \infty)$ is

$$- P_\star(v)y_\star(v) \int_t^v \xi_s ds \tag{4.2}$$

and we wish to maximise

$$U_t = \mathbb{E}_t \int_t^\infty \beta(t, v)u\left(e_v + P_\star(v)\xi_v - P_\star(v)y_\star(v)\int_t^v \xi_s ds\right) dv$$

$$= \int_t^\infty G(v, f(v), f'(v))dv, \tag{4.3}$$

where

$$f(v) := \int_t^v \xi_s ds, \tag{4.4}$$

$$f'(v) := \xi_v, \tag{4.5}$$

$$G(v, f, f') := \beta(t, v)\mathbb{E}_t\left[u\left(e_v + P_\star(v)f' - P_\star(v)y_\star(v)f\right)\right].$$

We assume that we use time t best estimates of the future distribution of $P_\star(v)$ and $y_\star(v)$ for $v \in [t, \infty)$ to calculate the expectation. If our joint probability density function for $P_\star(v) = x$ and $y_\star(v) = y$ at time t is $g(v, x, y)$ then U_t is a deterministic function of the envisaged trading strategy ξ_v as follows:

$$U_t = \int_t^\infty \int_{-\infty}^\infty \int_0^\infty \beta(t, v) \cdot \tag{4.6}$$

$$u\left(e_v + x\xi_v - xy \int_t^v \xi_s ds\right) g(v, x, y) dx dy dv.$$

If everything is well-behaved and sufficiently smooth, we can employ calculus of variations to maximise U_t over all possible trading strategies $\xi_v \in \mathbb{R}$ for $v \in [t, \infty)$ which gives for all $v \geq t$:

$$\frac{d}{dv}\left(\frac{\partial G}{\partial f'}\right) = \frac{\partial G}{\partial f}, \tag{4.7}$$

$$\frac{d}{dv}\left\{\beta(t, v)\mathbb{E}_t\left[u'(c_v) P_\star(v)\right]\right\} = -\beta(t, v)\mathbb{E}_t\left[u'(c_v) P_\star(v)y_\star(v)\right]$$

from which we obtain the pricing equation

$$\frac{\beta(t, T)\mathbb{E}_t\left[u'(c_T) P_\star(T)\right]}{u'(c_t)P_\star(t)} \tag{4.8}$$

$$= \exp\left(-\int_t^T \frac{\mathbb{E}_t\left[u'(c_v) P_\star(v)y_\star(v)\right]}{\mathbb{E}_t\left[u'(c_v) P_\star(v)\right]} dv\right).$$

4.2   Instantaneous Forward Yields

If we let $B^{\$}(t,T)$ denote the time t price of a time $T \geq t$ maturity US dollar zero coupon bond with $B^{\$}(T,T) = \$1$ then the value of this bond denominated in RUE at time t is $B^{\$}(t,T)P_{\$}(t)$. Being a zero coupon bond means that it accrues zero Net Income Yield. Applying the pricing equation (4.8) to this RUE denominated asset and $P_{\$}$ respectively gives

$$u'(c_t)B^{\$}(t,T)P_{\$}(t) \tag{4.9}$$

$$= \beta(t,T)\mathbb{E}_t\left[u'\left(c_T\right)B^{\$}(T,T)P_{\$}(T)\right]$$

and

$$\frac{\beta(t,T)\mathbb{E}_t\left[u'\left(c_T\right)P_{\$}(T)\right]}{u'(c_t)P_{\$}(t)} \tag{4.10}$$

$$= \exp\left(-\int_t^T \frac{\mathbb{E}_t\left[u'\left(c_v\right)P_{\$}(v)y_{\$}(v)\right]}{\mathbb{E}_t\left[u'\left(c_v\right)P_{\$}(v)\right]}dv\right).$$

Combining equations (4.9) and (4.10) tells us that

$$\log B^{\$}(t,T) \;=\; -\int_t^T \frac{\mathbb{E}_t\left[u'\left(c_v\right)P_{\$}(v)y_{\$}(v)\right]}{\mathbb{E}_t\left[u'\left(c_v\right)P_{\$}(v)\right]}dv. \tag{4.11}$$

So the time t instantaneous forward rate $f^{\$}(t, T)$ for a US dollar zero coupon bond maturing at time T is given by

$$\int_t^T f^{\$}(t, v)dv \quad := \quad -\log B^{\$}(t, T), \tag{4.12}$$

$$f^{\$}(t, v) \quad = \quad \frac{\mathbb{E}_t\left[u'(c_v) P_{\$}(v)y_{\$}(v)\right]}{\mathbb{E}_t\left[u'(c_v) P_{\$}(v)\right]}. \tag{4.13}$$

This relationship holds generally for the instantaneous forward rates of zero coupon bonds that pay any asset. For example, if $f^{\star}(t, T)$ is the instantaneous forward rate for a general asset $P_{\star}$ zero coupon bond then

$$f^{\star}(t, v) \quad = \quad \frac{\mathbb{E}_t\left[u'(c_v) P_{\star}(v)y_{\star}(v)\right]}{\mathbb{E}_t\left[u'(c_v) P_{\star}(v)\right]}. \tag{4.14}$$

In particular, we know that the Net Income Yield for the Market portfolio is identically zero, $y_M \equiv 0$. It follows from equation (4.14) that spot and forward yields on the Market portfolio are identically zero, with $f^M(t, v) \equiv 0$.

4.3   Forward Prices

The following analysis generalises to any pair of currencies or assets. Let $P_{\$}$ denote USD/RUE, the price of US dollars denominated in RUE, and $P_{\pounds}$ denote GBP/RUE, the price of Pounds sterling denominated in RUE. We know from equations (4.9) and (4.10) that

$$\frac{\beta(t,T)\mathbb{E}_t\left[u'(c_T)P_{\$}(T)\right]}{u'(c_t)P_{\$}(t)} \tag{4.15}$$

$$= \exp\left(-\int_t^T \frac{\mathbb{E}_t\left[u'(c_v)\,P_{\$}(v)y_{\$}(v)\right]}{\mathbb{E}_t\left[u'(c_v)\,P_{\$}(v)\right]}dv\right)$$

$$= B^{\$}(t,T),$$

and

$$\frac{\beta(t,T)\mathbb{E}_t\left[u'(c_T)P_{\pounds}(T)\right]}{u'(c_t)P_{\pounds}(t)} \tag{4.16}$$

$$= \exp\left(-\int_t^T \frac{\mathbb{E}_t\left[u'(c_v)\,P_{\pounds}(v)y_{\pounds}(v)\right]}{\mathbb{E}_t\left[u'(c_v)\,P_{\pounds}(v)\right]}dv\right)$$

$$= B^{\pounds}(t,T),$$

where $y_{\$}$ and $y_{\pounds}$ are the Net Income Yields for the US dollar and British pound assets respectively, and $B^{\$}(t,T)$ and $B^{\pounds}(t,T)$ are the US dollar and sterling denominated prices of US dollar and sterling zero coupon bonds respectively. So

$$\frac{P_£(t)}{P_\$(t)} \cdot \frac{\mathbb{E}_t \left[u'(c_T) P_\$(T) \right]}{\mathbb{E}_t \left[u'(c_T) P_£(T) \right]} = \frac{B^\$(t,T)}{B^£(t,T)}. \qquad (4.17)$$

Denote the GBP/USD spot exchange rate by $F(t,t) := P_£(t)/P_\$(t)$ and the GBP/USD forward exchange rate for future time T known at time t by $F(t,T) \in \mathcal{F}_t$. At time t we can engage in a forward contract to exchange one British pound for US dollars at time T at rate $F(t,T)$. Doing this we obtain

$$\frac{\mathbb{E}_t \left[u'(c_T) P_£(T) \right]}{\mathbb{E}_t \left[u'(c_T) P_\$(T) \right]} = \frac{\mathbb{E}_t \left[u'(c_T) F(t,T) P_\$(T) \right]}{\mathbb{E}_t \left[u'(c_T) P_\$(T) \right]} \qquad (4.18)$$

$$= F(t,T).$$

Comparing this with equation (4.17) gives the usual relationship:

$$F(t,T) = F(t,t) \cdot \frac{B^£(t,T)}{B^\$(t,T)}. \qquad (4.19)$$

It is clear that

$$F(t,T) = \frac{\mathbb{E}_t \left[u'(c_T) P_£(T) \right]}{\mathbb{E}_t \left[u'(c_T) P_\$(T) \right]}, \qquad (4.20)$$

$$\mathbb{E}_t[F(T,T)] = \mathbb{E}_t \left[\frac{u'(c_T) P_£(T)}{u'(c_T) P_\$(T)} \right], \qquad (4.21)$$

and in particular,

$$F(t, T) \;=\; \frac{\mathbb{E}_t\left[u'(c_T)P_\$(T)F(T,T)\right]}{\mathbb{E}_t\left[u'(c_T)P_\$(T)\right]}. \qquad (4.22)$$

So

$$F(t,T) - \mathbb{E}_t[F(T,T)] \qquad (4.23)$$

$$= \frac{1}{\mathbb{E}_t\left[u'(c_T)P_\$(T)\right]} \cdot \mathbb{COV}_t\left[u'(c_T)P_\$(T), \frac{P_\pounds(T)}{P_\$(T)}\right]$$

$$\not\equiv \; 0.$$

Forward foreign exchange rates are therefore biased predictors of spot foreign exchange rates.

This result applies to all assets. For example, if we substitute the Market portfolio for GBP then $F(t,t)$ and $F(t,T)$ become the US dollar denominated spot and forward prices of the Market portfolio, respectively. It is generally true that forward prices (denominated in any risky base currency) are biased predictors of future spot prices.

CAPM & Systematic Risk

The Capital Asset Pricing Model (CAPM) (Treynor [9], Sharpe [8], Lintner [4], Mossin [7]) is a model that arises from Modern Portfolio Theory (Markowitz [5]). Modern Portfolio Theory specifies a mean-variance efficient frontier for optimal investment that is linear in the presence of a risk-free asset, and includes the risk-free asset as the optimal investment with zero risk. CAPM says that if all market participants invest in mean-variance efficient portfolios, the Market portfolio will also be on this frontier, so the expected return of any asset will be a weighted average of the risk-free return and the return on the Market portfolio.

5.1   CAPM in RUE

From the perspective of this book, Modern Portfolio Theory is sensitive to base currency choice because this choice arbitrarily defines the risk-free asset. This problem can be avoided by applying Modern Portfolio Theory and CAPM denominated in RUE. However, another criticism that remains is that mean-variance optimisation lacks the generality of models based on general utility functions.

To see that CAPM is a special case of the consumption-based pricing equation (4.8) we first apply the pricing equation to a zero coupon bond $B^\star(t, T)$ paying out one unit of a general asset $P_\star$ at maturity at time T. This bond has RUE price $P_\star(t)B^\star(t, T)$ at time t giving

$$B^\star(t, T)u'(c_t)P_\star(t) \quad = \quad \beta(t, T)\mathbb{E}_t\left[u'\left(c_T\right)P_\star(T)\right]. \quad (5.1)$$

Rearranging this gives

$$B^\star(t,T) \;=\; \beta(t,T)\mathbb{E}_t\left[\frac{u'\left(c_T\right)}{u'(c_t)}\cdot\frac{P_\star(T)}{P_\star(t)}\right] \qquad (5.2)$$

$$=\; \beta(t,T)\mathbb{COV}_t\left[\frac{u'\left(c_T\right)}{u'(c_t)},\frac{P_\star(T)}{P_\star(t)}\right] +$$

$$\beta(t,T)\mathbb{E}_t\left[\frac{u'\left(c_T\right)}{u'(c_t)}\right]\mathbb{E}_t\left[\frac{P_\star(T)}{P_\star(t)}\right].$$

Applying the pricing equation (4.8) to a RUE zero coupon bond with price $B(t,T)$ paying out 1 RUE at time T gives

$$B(t,T)u'(c_t) \;=\; \beta(t,T)\mathbb{E}_t\left[u'\left(c_T\right)\right]. \qquad (5.3)$$

Combining this with equation (5.2) gives

$$\mathbb{E}_t\left[\frac{P_\star(T)}{P_\star(t)}\right] \;=\; \frac{B^\star(t,T)}{B(t,T)} - \qquad (5.4)$$

$$\frac{1}{B(t,T)}\mathbb{COV}_t\left[\frac{P_\star(T)}{P_\star(t)},\Lambda(t,T)\right],$$

where we define

$$\Lambda(t,T) \;:=\; \beta(t,T)\frac{u'(c_T)}{u'(c_t)}. \qquad (5.5)$$

If we now approximate $\Lambda(t, T)$ as a linear function of the performance of the Market portfolio with time-varying coefficients $a(t, T) \in \mathbb{R}$ and $b(t, T) \in \mathbb{R}$ both adapted to the filtration $\mathcal{F}_t$ then

$$\Lambda(t, T) \;=\; a(t, T) + b(t, T)\frac{M(T)}{M(t)}. \tag{5.6}$$

Applying this to the time t pricing of a RUE zero coupon bond paying out 1 RUE at time T then equation (5.3) gives

$$B(t, T) \;=\; a(t, T) + b(t, T)\mathbb{E}_t\left[\frac{M(T)}{M(t)}\right]. \tag{5.7}$$

Applying the pricing equation (4.8) to the Market portfolio and recalling that it has zero Net Income Yield gives

$$1 \;=\; \mathbb{E}_t\left[\frac{M(T)}{M(t)}\cdot\Lambda(t, T)\right] \tag{5.8}$$

$$\;=\; a(t, T)\mathbb{E}_t\left[\frac{M(T)}{M(t)}\right] + b(t, T)\mathbb{E}_t\left(\frac{M(T)}{M(t)}\right)^2. \tag{5.9}$$

So

$$a(t, T) \;=\; \frac{B(t, T)\mathbb{E}_t\left[M(T)/M(t)\right]^2 - \mathbb{E}_t\left[M(T)/M(t)\right]}{\mathrm{VAR}_t\left[M(T)/M(t)\right]},$$

$$b(t, T) \;=\; \frac{1 - B(t, T)\mathbb{E}_t\left[M(T)/M(t)\right]}{\mathrm{VAR}_t\left[M(T)/M(t)\right]}.$$

Substituting for $\Lambda(t,T)$ in equation (5.4) gives the usual CAPM relationship denominated in RUE as follows:

$$\mathbb{E}_t\left[\frac{P_\star(T)}{P_\star(t)}\right] = \frac{B^\star(t,T)}{B(t,T)} - \tag{5.10}$$

$$\frac{1}{B(t,T)}\mathrm{COV}_t\left[\frac{P_\star(T)}{P_\star(t)}, a(t,T) + b(t,T)\frac{M(T)}{M(t)}\right]$$

$$= \frac{B^\star(t,T)}{B(t,T)} + \tag{5.11}$$

$$\left(\mathbb{E}_t\left[\frac{M(T)}{M(t)}\right] - \frac{1}{B(t,T)}\right)\beta_{CAPM}(P_\star, M),$$

where $\beta_{CAPM}(P_\star, M)$ is the ordinary least squares beta (slope) coefficient of the performance of the asset $P_\star$ against the performance of the Market portfolio:

$$\beta_{CAPM}(P_\star, M) := \mathrm{COV}_t\left[\frac{P_\star(T)}{P_\star(t)}, \frac{M(T)}{M(t)}\right]/\mathrm{VAR}_t\left[\frac{M(T)}{M(t)}\right].$$

We later discover that there is a high empirical correlation between USD/RUE and US consumption denominated in RUE. Recall from equation (5.5) that $\Lambda(t,T)$ is a function of consumption. This means that it ought to be far more appropriate to approximate $\Lambda(t,T)$ as a linear function of USD/RUE than of the Market portfolio. So let us repeat the derivation of CAPM but this time using a linear function of USD/RUE to approximate $\Lambda(t, T)$ as follows:

$$\Lambda(t, T) \;=\; a(t, T) + b(t, T)\frac{P_\$(T)}{P_\$(t)}. \qquad (5.12)$$

Fitting the coefficients $a(t, T)$ and $b(t, T)$ as before, using the pricing equation (4.8) for a RUE zero coupon bond and the US dollar asset, we obtain

$$a(t, T) \;=\; \frac{B(t, T)\mathbb{E}_t\left[P_\$(T)/P_\$(t)\right]^2 - \mathbb{E}_t\left[P_\$(T)/P_\$(t)\right]}{\mathbb{V}\mathbb{A}\mathbb{R}_t\left[P_\$(T)/P_\$(t)\right]},$$

$$b(t, T) \;=\; \frac{B^\$(t, T) - B(t, T)\mathbb{E}_t\left[P_\$(T)/P_\$(t)\right]}{\mathbb{V}\mathbb{A}\mathbb{R}_t\left[P_\$(T)/P_\$(t)\right]}.$$

This gives a modified version of CAPM under RUE:

$$\mathbb{E}_t\left[\frac{P_\star(T)}{P_\star(t)}\right] \;=\; \frac{B^\star(t, T)}{B(t, T)} + \qquad (5.13)$$

$$\left(\mathbb{E}_t\left[\frac{P_\$(T)}{P_\$(t)}\right] - \frac{B^\$(t, T)}{B(t, T)}\right)\beta_{CAPM}(P_\star, P_\$),$$

where we use USD/RUE in place of the Market portfolio.

This RUE denominated CAPM suggests that USD/RUE is systematic risk, with striking implications for US dollar denominated risk and return. What US dollar denominated theory considers risk-free cash is actually pure systematic risk!

5.2 US Dollar Illusion

We now show that to the extent that the above is not true and USD/RUE is not systematic risk, USD/RUE would instead appear as illusory systematic risk under any US dollar denominated theory.

Consider the quadratic variation of the US dollar denominated price of the general asset $P_\star$, via Itô

$$\left\langle \frac{d[P_\star/P_\$]}{P_\star/P_\$} \right\rangle = \left\langle \frac{dP_\star}{P_\star} \right\rangle + \left\langle \frac{dP_\$}{P_\$} \right\rangle - \quad (5.14)$$

$$2\left\langle \frac{dP_\star}{P_\star}, \frac{dP_\$}{P_\$} \right\rangle .$$

Now suppose that $P_\star$ is the RUE price of a diversified portfolio with a beta of one to systematic risk, and that idiosyncratic risk has been diversified away. If systematic risk is uncorrelated with USD/RUE then

$$\left\langle \frac{d[P_\star/P_\$]}{P_\star/P_\$} \right\rangle = \left\langle \frac{dP_\star}{P_\star} \right\rangle + \left\langle \frac{dP_\$}{P_\$} \right\rangle , \quad (5.15)$$

so USD/RUE risk contributes to the US dollar denominated volatility of systematic risk (i.e. systematic risk denominated in US dollars).

Alternatively if USD/RUE is actually systematic risk then from a US dollar denominated perspective systematic risk disappears,

$$\left\langle \frac{d[P_\star/P_\$]}{P_\star/P_\$} \right\rangle = 0. \tag{5.16}$$

USD/RUE is therefore an illusory undiversifiable systematic risk denominated in US dollars if it is not already genuine systematic risk under the unbiased perspective of RUE. Perversely, the more US dollar cash resembles genuine systematic risk, the more it hides from US dollar denominated observations of systematic risk.

Note that we do not propose that any version of CAPM actually holds as it is only one of many possible special cases of the general consumption-based pricing equation. But if we must use CAPM then the above analysis and empirical evidence suggest that US dollar cash may be a reasonable approximation to systematic risk.

— 6 —

Utility Transformations

Using the consumption-based asset pricing model we here offer a risk-neutral version of the RUE framework under which the pricing equation takes a simplified form. We show that logarithmic utility either holds under all possible choices of base currency, or does not hold anywhere. We also show that consumption-based asset pricing fails if the base currency asset is perfectly correlated with consumption and log-utility does not hold. This result is relevant to our later analysis of the US Equity Risk Premium Puzzle.

6.1   Risk-Neutral RUE (RNR)

The RUE framework attributes risk between assets, and risk preferences are captured by the utility function u. Here we present a useful alternative price framework that we call 'Risk-Neutral RUE', or RNR for short. We define RNR by specifying the RUE/RNR exchange rate process $X(t) := u'(c_t) > 0$ which tells us the number of RNR per 1 RUE.

Recall that ratios of exchange are unaffected by multiplication of RUE prices by a general process $X(t) > 0$ so if $\tilde{P}_i(t) := P_i(t)X(t)$ is the RNR price of basis asset i for each $i \in \{0, 1, \ldots, N\}$, the ratio of exchange property continues to hold for RNR prices as follows: $E_{ij}(t) = P_i(t)/P_j(t) = \tilde{P}_i(t)/\tilde{P}_j(t)$ for all $i, j \in \{0, 1, \ldots, N\}$.

Applying the pricing equation (4.8) to a basis asset i zero coupon bond $B^i(t, T)$ with RUE price $P_i(t)B^i(t, T)$ at time t and paying one unit of asset i at time T gives

$$B^i(t, T)u'(c_t)P_i(t) \;=\; \beta(t, T)\mathbb{E}_t\left[u'(c_T)\,P_i(T)\right]. \quad (6.1)$$

Comparing this with the pricing equation (4.8) applied to basis asset i tells us that

$$B^i(t, T) \;=\; \exp\left(-\int_t^T \frac{\mathbb{E}_t\left[u'(c_v)\,P_i(v)y_i(v)\right]}{\mathbb{E}_t\left[u'(c_v)\,P_i(v)\right]}dv\right). \quad (6.2)$$

The primary motivation for RNR is that this relationship then simplifies to

$$\tilde{P}_i(t) \quad = \quad \frac{\beta(t,T)}{B^i(t,T)} \cdot \mathbb{E}[\tilde{P}_i(T)|\mathcal{F}_t], \tag{6.3}$$

$$B^i(t,T) \quad = \quad \exp\left(-\int_t^T \frac{\mathbb{E}_t[\tilde{P}_i(v)y_i(v)]}{\mathbb{E}_t[\tilde{P}_i(v)]}dv\right). \tag{6.4}$$

This property is sufficiently simple that direct estimation of USD/RNR from US dollar prices using this relationship may be easier than separate estimation of USD/RUE and the utility function u, as knowledge of RNR conveniently avoids the need to know the utility function.

In terms of ratios of exchange equation (6.3) tells us that

$$E_{ij}(t) = \frac{\tilde{P}_i(t)}{\tilde{P}_j(t)} = \frac{\mathbb{E}_t[\tilde{P}_i(T)]/B^i(t,T)}{\mathbb{E}_t[\tilde{P}_j(T)]/B^j(t,T)}. \tag{6.5}$$

Similarly, the forward ratio of exchange $E_{ij}(t,T) \in \mathcal{F}_t$ of $E_{ij}(T)$, known at time t, is given by

$$E_{ij}(t,T) = E_{ij}(t) \cdot \frac{B^i(t,T)}{B^j(t,T)} = \frac{\mathbb{E}_t[\tilde{P}_i(T)]}{\mathbb{E}_t[\tilde{P}_j(T)]}. \tag{6.6}$$

Given that $E_{ij}(t) = E_{ij}(t,t)$, the relationship

$$E_{ij}(t, v) = \mathbb{E}_t[\tilde{P}_i(v)]/\mathbb{E}_t[\tilde{P}_j(v)] \tag{6.7}$$

neatly summarises how spot and forward ratios of exchange are easily obtained from price processes under the RNR numeraire.

The utility function u applied to RUE prices is equivalent to identity utility applied to RNR prices. One way of thinking about the distinction between RUE and RNR is that multiplying RUE prices by $X(t) = u'(c_t)$ changes the decomposition of risk and return between assets from what is most statistically justifiable (RUE price dynamics), to what results in risk-neutrality (RNR price dynamics). Of course, it is possible for RUE and RNR to coincide if identity utility holds under RUE.

6.2   Invariant Utility

Multiplying RUE prices by the RUE/RNR exchange rate process $X(t) = u'(c_t)$ maps RUE prices to a world where identity utility can be used in the pricing equation (4.8). Now consider a general exchange rate process $X(t) > 0$ that maps RUE prices to a new version of RUE, denoted RUE-X, where the pricing equation (4.8) continues to hold provided the utility function $\nu : \mathbb{R} \to \mathbb{R}$ is used instead of u.

The RUE price $P_i(t)$ of basis asset i has RUE-X price $\tilde{P}_i(t) :=$ $P_i(t)X(t)$. As before, the ratio of exchange property continues to hold for RUE-X prices with $E_{ij}(t) = \tilde{P}_i(t)/\tilde{P}_j(t)$.

Recall that the pricing equation (4.8) for basis asset i in RUE gives

$$B^i(t, T)u'(c_t)P_i(t) \;=\; \beta(t, T)\mathbb{E}_t\left[u'(c_T)\,P_i(T)\right], \qquad (6.8)$$

$$B^i(t, T) \;=\; \exp\left(-\int_t^T \frac{\mathbb{E}_t\left[u'(c_v)\,P_i(v)y_i(v)\right]}{\mathbb{E}_t\left[u'(c_v)\,P_i(v)\right]}dv\right).$$

The same pricing equation using RUE-X prices (remembering that the RUE-X utility function ν is a function of RUE-X denominated consumption) gives

$$B^i(t,T)\nu'(c_t X(t))P_i(t)X(t) \tag{6.9}$$

$$= \beta(t,T)\mathbb{E}_t\left[\nu'\left(c_T X(T)\right)P_i(T)X(T)\right],$$

$$B^i(t,T) \tag{6.10}$$

$$= \exp\left(-\int_t^T \frac{\mathbb{E}_t\left[\nu'\left(c_v X(v)\right)P_i(v)X(v)y_i(v)\right]}{\mathbb{E}_t\left[\nu'\left(c_v X(v)\right)P_i(v)X(v)\right]}dv\right).$$

So for consistency of asset pricing under RUE and RUE-X we require

$$u'(c_t) \equiv \nu'(c_t X(t))X(t). \tag{6.11}$$

If $X(t) = u'(c_t)$ then $\nu'(c_t u'(c_t)) \equiv 1$ so identity utility $\nu(x) = x$ will give consistent pricing under this RUE-X which is equivalent to RNR. If log-utility holds under RUE with $u(x) = \log x$, then taking $X(t) = u'(c_t)$ gives $1 = \nu'(1)$ which is true of any utility function ν because utility functions are equivalent up to linear transformations and consumption is constant denominated in this particular RUE-X numeraire. So identity utility $\nu(x) = x$ and log-utility $\nu(x) = \log x$ will both provide consistent pricing under RNR if log-utility holds under RUE.

For general $X(t)$, if log-utility holds under RUE with $u'(c_t) = 1/c_t$ then equation (6.11) tells us that log-utility also holds under RUE-X, with $\nu'(c_t X(t)) = 1/(c_t X(t))$. Similarly, if log-utility holds under RUE-X with $\nu'(x) = 1/x$, equation (6.11) tells us that log-utility also holds under RUE. It follows that if log-utility holds under any numeraire, then log-utility holds under all numeraires. Log-utility is invariant to choice of base currency.

6.3   Asset Pricing Failure Under US Dollars

If $X(t) := 1/P_\$(t)$ then RUE-X is equivalent to US dollar prices. Equation (6.11) becomes

$$u'(c_t) \quad \equiv \quad \nu'(c_t/P_\$(t))/P_\$(t). \tag{6.12}$$

So if log-utility holds under RUE, log-utility also holds denominated in US dollars. Similarly, if log-utility holds denominated in US dollars then log-utility also holds under RUE.

Now consider the RUE-X numeraire defined by $X(t) = 1/c_t$. Equation (6.11) tells that $u'(c_t)c_t = \nu'(1)$. If u is log-utility then this RUE-X is RNR. Otherwise, there does not exist an equivalent utility function ν under this RUE-X. So either log-utility holds, or there exist numeraires under which no equivalent utility function holds.

So $X(t) = 1/c_t$ results in a RUE-X numeraire without an equivalent utility function ν unless log-utility holds. Now consider the possibility that $c_t \propto P_\$(t)$. This gives $X(t) = 1/c_t \propto 1/P_\$$ telling us that US dollar prices are a RUE-X numeraire under which no equivalent utility function holds, unless log-utility holds. In the event that log-utility holds, US dollar prices are RNR.

We later find that US consumption (denominated in RUE) and USD/RUE are highly correlated, so US dollar prices are an approximation to a numeraire under which consumption-based pricing does not work unless log-utility holds.

$$- 7 -$$

Estimating USD/RUE

USD/RUE, denoted $P_\$$, is the RUE price of one US dollar. Here we attempt to estimate USD/RUE empirically. Once USD/RUE is known, all other RUE prices can be found by multiplying US dollar prices by USD/RUE.

The following techniques only consider covariances and so only estimate USD/RUE up to an unknown drift rate. This unknown drift tends to cancel out when we map RUE prices back to US dollars or consider relative drift rates such as risk premia. Given that we do not estimate drifts here we choose to set the drift of our estimates of USD/RUE to zero.

7.1   Minimum Trace Method

The idea behind this approach is that the sum of the variances of the basis assets is minimised when denominated in the RUE numeraire versus any other numeraire (asymptotically as the number of assets tends to infinity). As an aide to intuition consider that correlated volatility in US dollar denominated prices contributes to the volatility of every asset, but would be attributed once to the US dollar asset under the RUE numeraire thus decreasing the sum of asset variances. The RUE numeraire is the numeraire where no additional risk has been added to prices in aggregate due to risk attributable to the numeraire.

A possible way to visualise this approach is to note that at each time t we know the RUE prices $p_i(t)$ of real-world assets $i \in \{1, 2, \ldots, N\}$ up to an unknown factor $P_\$(t)$. Plotting the points $(t, \log p_i(t)) = (t, \log p_i^\$(t) + \log P_\$(t))$ on a chart, where $p_i^\$(t)$ is the US dollar price of real-world asset $i \in \{1, 2, \ldots, N\}$ at time $t \in [0, T]$, illustrates that choosing $P_\$(t)$ shifts the pattern of points up or down for that time t. The Minimum Trace Method chooses to shift the points up and down at each time t to minimise the total sum of the squares of the consecutive misalignments of each asset's estimated log RUE price between time steps. In contrast, US dollar prices are aligned so that the points representing the log-returns of the US dollar asset fall on the x-axis at every time t.

Let us define the function

$$H(X) \ := \ \sum_{i=1}^{N} \left\langle \frac{d(A_i X/P_\$)}{A_i X/P_\$} \right\rangle / dt. \qquad (7.1)$$

The value of $H(P_\$)$ is the sum of the variances of the basis assets denominated in the RUE numeraire. We then calculate via Itô

$$H(X) \cdot dt \ = \ \sum_{i=1}^{N} \left\langle \frac{dA_i}{A_i} + \frac{dX}{X} - \frac{dP_\$}{P_\$} \right\rangle \qquad (7.2)$$

$$= \ H(P_\$) + \qquad (7.3)$$

$$N \left\langle \frac{dX}{X} - \frac{dP_\$}{P_\$} \right\rangle + 2 \left\langle \sum_{i=1}^{N} \frac{dA_i}{A_i}, \frac{dX}{X} - \frac{dP_\$}{P_\$} \right\rangle.$$

So for any given X

$$\lim_{N\to\infty} \frac{H(X)}{N} \cdot dt = \left\langle \frac{dX}{X} - \frac{dP_\$}{P_\$} \right\rangle + \tag{7.4}$$

$$2 \lim_{N\to\infty} \left\langle \frac{1}{N} \sum_{i=1}^{N} \frac{dA_i}{A_i}, \frac{dX}{X} - \frac{dP_\$}{P_\$} \right\rangle$$

$$= \left\langle \frac{dX}{X} - \frac{dP_\$}{P_\$} \right\rangle, \tag{7.5}$$

provided the variance of an equal weighted portfolio of orthogonal basis assets (with constant holdings in the basis assets) tends to zero as the number of basis assets tends to infinity. So $H(X)$ is minimised by taking

$$\frac{dX}{X} = \frac{dP_\$}{P_\$} + \text{drift terms} \tag{7.6}$$

asymptotically as N tends to infinity. If P_e is our estimate of $P_\$$ the Minimum Trace Method chooses to set

$$P_e := \arg\min_X H(X). \tag{7.7}$$

This estimates $dP_\$/P_\$$ up to unknown drift terms. We then set the drift of our estimate to zero.

Let $\mathbf{V} \in \mathbb{R}^{N \times N}$ be the covariance matrix of N of the $N + 1$ real-world assets denominated in RUE, discarding the real-world asset lacking volatility denominated in RUE should one exist. The matrix $\mathbf{V}$ is symmetric positive-definite and so an orthogonal matrix $\mathbf{Q} \in \mathbb{R}^{N \times N}$ exists such that $\mathbf{V} = \mathbf{Q}\mathbf{D}\mathbf{Q}^T$ where $\mathbf{D} \in \mathbb{R}^{N \times N}$ is diagonal. It then follows by standard linear algebra that the trace of $\mathbf{V}$ equals the trace of $\mathbf{D}$, $tr(\mathbf{V}) = tr(\mathbf{D})$.

We define the risky components of our basis assets so that they have diagonal covariance matrix $\mathbf{D}$. The risky basis assets can therefore be thought of as the result of a principal components analysis decomposition.

If real-world asset i has a constant holding $h_{ij} \in \mathbb{R}$ in basis asset j then

$$p_i = \sum_{j=0}^{N} h_{ij} P_j, \tag{7.8}$$

$$dp_i = \sum_{j=0}^{N} h_{ij} dP_j, \tag{7.9}$$

$$\frac{dp_i}{p_i} = \sum_{j=0}^{N} \frac{h_{ij} P_j}{p_i} \frac{dP_j}{P_j} \tag{7.10}$$

$$= \sum_{j=0}^{N} w_{ij} \frac{dP_j}{P_j}, \tag{7.11}$$

where we denote the weight real-world asset i holds in basis asset j by $w_{ij} := h_{ij} P_j / p_i$. Then

$$(\mathbf{D})_{ij} = \left\langle \frac{dP_i}{P_i}, \frac{dP_j}{P_j} \right\rangle / dt = \sigma_i^2 \delta_{ij}, \tag{7.12}$$

$$(\mathbf{V})_{ij} = \left\langle \sum_{k=0}^{N} w_{ik} \frac{dP_k}{P_k}, \sum_{m=0}^{N} w_{jm} \frac{dP_m}{P_m} \right\rangle / dt \tag{7.13}$$

$$= \sum_{k=1}^{N} \sum_{m=1}^{N} w_{ik} w_{jm} (\mathbf{D})_{km}, \tag{7.14}$$

so we know that $\mathbf{V} = \mathbf{W}\mathbf{D}\mathbf{W}^T$ where we define the matrix $\mathbf{W} \in \mathbb{R}^{N \times N}$ elementwise by $(\mathbf{W})_{ij} = w_{ij}$ for $i, j \in \{1, 2, \ldots, N\}$.

Comparison with the principal components decomposition suggests we can interpret $\mathbf{Q}$ as the matrix of weights $\mathbf{W}$. Note that the weights in this matrix will not generally add up to one because the matrix $\mathbf{W}$ does not include the weights w_{ij} for $i, j \in \{0, 1, \ldots, N\}$ where either i or j is zero[1].

The quantity $H(P_\$)$ is the sum of the variances of the basis assets, which equals the trace of the covariance matrix, $tr(\mathbf{V})$. Traces of covariance matrices are invariant to change of basis. So the RUE numeraire can be estimated as the numeraire that minimises the sum of the variances of our real-world assets without us needing to worry about change of basis. We numerically estimate USD/RUE by minimising the trace of the covariance matrix of real-world asset returns denominated in our estimate of RUE.

Recall that $p_i^\$(t)$ is the US dollar price of real-world asset $i \in$

---

[1]Overall there are $(N + 1)^2$ weights w_{ij} for $i, j \in \{0, 1, \ldots, N\}$. Taking $\mathbf{W} = \mathbf{Q}$ tells us N^2 of these weights. Requiring weights to add to one for each real-world asset tells us an additional $N + 1$ weights, leaving us with N unknowns representing the unknown weights the discarded real-world asset holds in the basis assets.

$\{1, 2, \ldots, N\}$ at time $t \in [0, T]$. Denote the US dollar denominated log-return x_{ij} of real-world asset i at time $t = j\Delta t$ where $\Delta t = T/J$ for some $J \in \mathbb{N}$ for $j \in \{1, 2, \ldots, J\}$ by

$$x_{ij} \;=\; \log p_i^{\$}(j\Delta t) - \log p_i^{\$}((j-1)\Delta t). \qquad (7.15)$$

We let $i = 0$ represent the US dollar asset with $x_{0j} \equiv 0$ for all $j \in \{1, 2, \ldots, J\}$. Let z_j be the log-returns of our estimate of USD/RUE,

$$z_j \;:=\; \log P_e(j\Delta t) - \log P_e((j-1)\Delta t). \qquad (7.16)$$

Our estimated RUE denominated log-return of asset i at time t is then

$$\log \left[p_i^{\$}(j\Delta t) P_e(j\Delta t) \right] - \log \left[p_i^{\$}((j-1)\Delta t) P_e((j-1)\Delta t) \right]$$

$$=\; x_{ij} + z_j.$$

So in order to minimise the sum of the variances of our RUE denominated assets, including the RUE denominated variance of the

US dollar asset, we minimise the quantity Θ given by

$$\Theta \;=\; \frac{1}{J-1} \sum_{i=0}^{N} \sum_{j=1}^{J} (x_{ij} + z_j - \bar{x}_i - \bar{z})^2 , \qquad (7.17)$$

where

$$\bar{x}_i := \frac{1}{J} \sum_{k=1}^{J} x_{ik}, \qquad \bar{z} := \frac{1}{J} \sum_{k=1}^{J} z_k . \qquad (7.18)$$

We choose to set $\bar{z} = 0$. Differentiating Θ with respect to z_m for each $m \in \{1, 2, \ldots, J\}$ and setting the partial derivatives $\partial\Theta/\partial z_m$ to zero then gives

$$z_m \;=\; \frac{1}{J} \sum_{j=1}^{J} \left(\frac{1}{N+1} \sum_{i=1}^{N} x_{ij} \right) - \qquad (7.19)$$

$$\frac{1}{N+1} \sum_{i=1}^{N} x_{im},$$

$$P_e(m\Delta t) \;=\; P_e((m-1)\Delta t) \cdot \exp(z_m) . \qquad (7.20)$$

7.2   Iterative Method

Here we offer an iterative method for estimating USD/RUE that is dependent on robustly estimating the composition of the risk-free asset A_0. We know that A_0 is instantaneously risk-free under RUE, so if we know the US dollar denominated value of the risk-free asset $A_0/P_\$$ we can estimate $P_\$$ up to unknown drift terms by

$$d \log P_\$ \quad = \quad -d \log \frac{A_0}{P_\$} + \text{drift terms.} \qquad (7.21)$$

The obvious problem with this approach is that we don't know the composition of the risk-free asset A_0 until we know $P_\$$. One possible solution is to use an iterative approach.

Let $P_e^{(n)}$ denote our estimate of $P_\$$ at the nth iteration and let $A_0^{(n)}$ denote our estimate of A_0 at the nth iteration by forming a minimum variance portfolio denominated in RUE using $P_e^{(n)}$ to estimate RUE prices. Consistent with our earlier notation we define

$$z_j^{(n)} \quad := \quad \log P_e^{(n)}(j\Delta t) - \log P_e^{(n)}((j-1)\Delta t), \quad (7.22)$$

and initialise with $z_j^{(0)} = 0$ for all $j \in \{1, 2, \ldots, J\}$.

Let $\mathbf{V}^{(n)}$ denote our estimate of the covariance matrix of the RUE denominated real-world assets $\mathbf{V}$ (including the US dollar asset) at iteration n, then we can estimate the element $(\mathbf{V}^{(n)})_{ij}$ using the usual covariance estimator for all $i, j \in \{0, 1, \ldots, N\}$:

$$\frac{1}{J-1} \sum_{k=1}^{J} (x_{ik} + z_k^{(n)})(x_{jk} + z_k^{(n)}) - \tag{7.23}$$

$$\frac{1}{J(J-1)} \left(\sum_{k=1}^{J} (x_{ik} + z_k^{(n)}) \right) \left(\sum_{k=1}^{J} (x_{jk} + z_k^{(n)}) \right).$$

We then find the column vector of weights $\check{\mathbf{w}} \in \mathbb{R}^{N+1}$ that minimises portfolio variance under RUE given by $\mathbf{w}^T \mathbf{V}^{(n)} \mathbf{w}$. We use a regularisation parameter $\lambda_1 \geq 0$ to avoid over-fitting. This is important to ensure our estimate of A_0 is a diversified portfolio. We also demand that the weights sum to one, $\mathbf{e}_{N+1}^T \check{\mathbf{w}} = 1$, where $\mathbf{e}_{N+1} \in \mathbb{R}^{N+1}$ is a column vector of ones. This motivates the following Lagrangian:

$$L = \frac{1}{2} \mathbf{w}^T \mathbf{V}^{(n)} \mathbf{w} + \frac{1}{2} \lambda_1 \mathbf{w}^T \mathbf{w} - \lambda_2 (\mathbf{e}_{N+1}^T \mathbf{w} - 1), \tag{7.24}$$

where $\lambda_2 \in \mathbb{R}$ is a Lagrange multiplier.

Minimising this gives

$$\left.\frac{\partial L}{\partial \mathbf{w}}\right|_{\mathbf{w}=\check{\mathbf{w}}} = \mathbf{V}^{(n)}\check{\mathbf{w}} + \lambda_1\check{\mathbf{w}} - \lambda_2 \mathbf{e}_{N+1} = 0, \qquad (7.25)$$

$$\check{\mathbf{w}} = \frac{[\lambda_1\mathbf{I}_{N+1} + \mathbf{V}^{(n)}]^{-1}\mathbf{e}_{N+1}}{\mathbf{e}_{N+1}^T[\lambda_1\mathbf{I}_{N+1} + \mathbf{V}^{(n)}]^{-1}\mathbf{e}_{N+1}}, \qquad (7.26)$$

where $\mathbf{I}_{N+1} \in \mathbb{R}^{(N+1)\times(N+1)}$ is an identity matrix.

If we denote the column vector of US dollar denominated real-world asset prices by $\mathbf{p}^{\$} \in \mathbb{R}^{N+1}$ with $(\mathbf{p}^{\$})_i = p_i^{\$}$ for $i \in \{1, 2, \dots, N\}$ and $(\mathbf{p}^{\$})_0 \equiv 1$ we can iterate as follows, using the expectation term to keep the drift of $d\log P_e^{(n)}$ constant:

$$d\log P_e^{(n+1)} := -d\log\frac{A_0^{(n)}}{P_e^{(n)}} + \mathbb{E}\left[d\log\frac{A_0^{(n)}}{P_e^{(n)}}\right], \qquad (7.27)$$

$$A_0^{(n)} := \frac{\mathbf{e}_{N+1}^T\left[\lambda_1\mathbf{I}_{N+1} + \mathbf{V}^{(n)}\right]^{-1}\mathbf{p}^{\$}}{\mathbf{e}_{N+1}^T\left[\lambda_1\mathbf{I}_{N+1} + \mathbf{V}^{(n)}\right]^{-1}\mathbf{e}_{N+1}}P_e^{(n)}.$$

So numerically, if $\mathbf{z}^{(n)} \in \mathbb{R}^J$ is a column vector defined by $(\mathbf{z}^{(n)})_j = z_j^{(n)}$ and $\mathbf{x} \in \mathbb{R}^{(N+1)\times J}$ is a matrix defined by $(\mathbf{x})_{ij} = x_{ij}$ for all $(i, j) \in \{1, 2, \dots, N\} \times \{1, 2, \dots, J\}$ with $(\mathbf{x})_{0j} = 0$ for all

$j \in \{1, 2, \ldots, J\}$ we estimate

$$\mathbf{z}^{(n+1)} \ := \ \left[\frac{\mathbf{e}_J^T \mathbf{e}_J}{J} - \mathbf{I}_J\right] \frac{\mathbf{x}^T \left[\lambda_1 \mathbf{I}_{N+1} + \mathbf{V}^{(n)}\right]^{-1} \mathbf{e}_{N+1}}{\mathbf{e}_{N+1}^T \left[\lambda_1 \mathbf{I}_{N+1} + \mathbf{V}^{(n)}\right]^{-1} \mathbf{e}_{N+1}},$$

where $\mathbf{e}_J \in \mathbb{R}^J$ is a column vector of ones, and $\mathbf{I}_J \in \mathbb{R}^{J \times J}$ is an identity matrix.

The Iterative Method can be considered a generalisation of the Minimum Trace Method, because as the regularisation parameter λ_1 tends to infinity, USD/RUE estimated by the Iterative Method tends to that estimated via the Minimum Trace Method.

$-$ 8 $-$

Equity Risk Premia Puzzle

Here we apply our estimates of USD/RUE to examine the US Equity Risk Premium Puzzle. We propose that the puzzle can be explained by the arbitrary definition of US dollars as the risk-free asset under the usual base currency approach, and high positive correlation between US consumption denominated in RUE and USD/RUE. We hypothesise that this correlation arises from widespread pegging of US salaries and budgets to US dollar denominated constants.

8.1   Equity Risk Premia Puzzle

In 1985, Mehra and Prescott [6] demonstrated that (using the language of modern finance with its usual US dollar centric perspective on risk) 'the return earned by a risky security in excess of that earned by a relatively risk-free T-bill was an order of magnitude greater than could be rationalised in the context of the standard neoclassical paradigms of financial economics, as a premium for bearing risk'. This became known as the Equity Risk Premium Puzzle.

Applying our pricing equation (4.8) to one unit of a general asset $P_\star$ with price $P_\star(t) \in \mathbb{R}$ at time t and Net Income Yield $y_\star(t) \in \mathbb{R}$ gives:

$$\frac{\beta(t,T)\mathbb{E}_t\left[u'\left(c_T\right)P_\star(T)\right]}{u'(c_t)P_\star(t)} \tag{8.1}$$

$$= \exp\left(-\int_t^T \frac{\mathbb{E}_t\left[u'\left(c_v\right)P_\star(v)y_\star(v)\right]}{\mathbb{E}_t\left[u'\left(c_v\right)P_\star(v)\right]}dv\right).$$

Applying the pricing equation to an asset $P_\star$ zero coupon bond $B^\star(t,T)$ with RUE price $P_\star(t)B^\star(t,T)$ at time t and paying one unit of asset $P_\star$ at time T gives

$$u'(c_t)P_\star(t)B^\star(t,T) = \beta(t,T)\mathbb{E}_t\left[u'\left(c_T\right)P_\star(T)B^\star(T,T)\right], \tag{8.2}$$

$$B^\star(t,T) = \exp\left(-\int_t^T \frac{\mathbb{E}_t\left[u'\left(c_v\right)P_\star(v)y_\star(v)\right]}{\mathbb{E}_t\left[u'\left(c_v\right)P_\star(v)\right]}dv\right).$$

For a RUE zero coupon bond $B(t, T)$ paying out 1 RUE at maturity the pricing equation gives

$$u'(c_t)B(t, T) \; = \; \beta(t, T)\mathbb{E}_t\left[u'(c_T)\right]. \tag{8.3}$$

From the definition of covariance it follows that

$$\mathbb{COV}_t\left[u'(c_T), \frac{P_\star(T)}{P_\star(t)}\right] \tag{8.4}$$

$$= \; \mathbb{E}_t\left[u'(c_T)\frac{P_\star(T)}{P_\star(t)}\right] - \mathbb{E}_t\left[u'(c_T)\right]\mathbb{E}_t\left[\frac{P_\star(T)}{P_\star(t)}\right] \tag{8.5}$$

$$= \; \frac{u'(c_t)}{\beta(t, T)}\left(B^\star(t, T) - B(t, T)\mathbb{E}_t\left[\frac{P_\star(T)}{P_\star(t)}\right]\right). \tag{8.6}$$

Rearranging and noting that correlations are in $[-1, 1]$ gives

$$\left|\mathbb{E}_t\left[\frac{P_\star(T)}{P_\star(t)}\right] - \frac{B^\star(t, T)}{B(t, T)}\right|/\text{stdev}\left(\frac{P_\star(T)}{P_\star(t)}\right) \tag{8.7}$$

$$\leq \; \frac{\text{stdev}\left(u'(c_T)\right)}{\mathbb{E}_t\left[u'(c_T)\right]},$$

where $\text{stdev}(X)$ denotes the standard deviation of X.

If a power utility function with constant relative risk aversion (CRRA) is assumed then $u'(x) = x^{-\gamma}$, where γ is the Arrow-Pratt measure of relative risk aversion. If we also assume that consumption growth is lognormal then:

$$dc_t/c_t := \mu_c dt + \sigma_c dW_c^*, \tag{8.8}$$

$$du'(c_t)/u'(c_t) = (-\gamma\mu_c + \gamma(1+\gamma)\sigma_c^2/2)dt - \tag{8.9}$$

$$\gamma\sigma_c dW_c^*,$$

$$\log \frac{u'(c_T)}{u'(c_t)} = \gamma \int_t^T (-\mu_c + \sigma_c^2/2)ds - \tag{8.10}$$

$$\gamma \int_t^T \sigma_c dW_c^*,$$

where μ_c and σ_c are the drift and volatility, respectively, of consumption that is driven by a Brownian motion W_c^*. Assuming constant drifts and volatilities, with the drift and volatility of asset $P_\star$ being $\mu_\star$ and $\sigma_\star$ respectively, and taking $T = t+1$, we then obtain

$$\frac{\text{stdev}\,(u'\,(c_T))}{\mathbb{E}_t\,[u'\,(c_T)]} \approx \gamma\sigma_c, \tag{8.11}$$

$$\text{stdev}\left(\frac{P_\star(T)}{P_\star(t)}\right) \approx \sigma_\star, \tag{8.12}$$

$$\mathbb{E}_t\left[\frac{P_\star(T)}{P_\star(t)}\right] \approx 1+\mu_\star. \tag{8.13}$$

The inequality (8.7) becomes

$$\left| 1 + \mu_\star - \frac{B^\star(t, t+1)}{B(t, t+1)} \right| / \sigma_\star \ \leq \ \gamma \sigma_c. \qquad (8.14)$$

If we set asset $P_\star$ to be a portfolio holding the S&P 500 with dividends reinvested then $B^\star(t, t+1) \equiv 1$ and the left hand side of equation (8.14) is recognisable as the Sharpe ratio of asset $P_\star$.

When equation (8.14) is applied (erroneously[1]) to the S&P 500 denominated in US dollars with reinvested dividends and using US dollar denominated zero coupon bonds, γ is found to be too high. In the 79 years from end 1929 to end 2008, the Sharpe ratio of the S&P 500 index denominated in US dollars with dividends reinvested has been 0.4. The standard deviation of US consumption per capita[2] denominated in US dollars over the same period has been 5.5%. This suggests risk-aversion $\gamma \geq 6.5$. This contrasts with research on investor behaviour that suggests that risk aversion is likely to be smaller and in the range 1-3 (Friend and Blume [3] estimated it to be larger than 1 on average and probably in excess of 2). This mismatch between US dollar denominated theory and

---

[1] Due to the implicit assumption that US dollars are risk-free.
[2] Not seasonally nor inflation adjusted. Sourced from the U.S. Bureau of Economic Analysis.

empirical evidence is the Equity Risk Premium Puzzle. The puzzle is made more extreme by the fact that the S&P 500 is unlikely to be on the efficient frontier, so there probably exist portfolios of assets that imply even higher risk aversion.

One of the possible explanations for the puzzle is luck. The time-spans over which the Sharpe ratio is typically measured, 50-100 years, are much shorter than those required to estimate drift rates with statistical significance. Another possible explanation is that US consumption is a poor proxy for the consumption of a global stand-in household. However, the failure to account for base currency risk in the US dollar denominated formulation of the Equity Risk Premium Puzzle is an oversight that introduces bias, independently of the problems that arise from statistical estimation and choice of stand-in consumption estimate.

Equation (8.14) is the formulation of the Equity Risk Premium puzzle in the RUE numeraire. Using the Minimum Trace and Iterative methods we estimate USD/RUE using annual data from end 1929 to end 2008. We use the CRSP S&P 500 universe value weighted and equal weighted indices with dividends reinvested[3], and 90 and 30 day Treasury bill indices. We then numerically find a time-series estimating USD/RUE using both the Minimum Trace Method and the Iterative Method with regularisation parameter $\lambda_1 = 1$.

We estimate $B(t, t+1) = 1/(1+R)$ in each case by taking R as

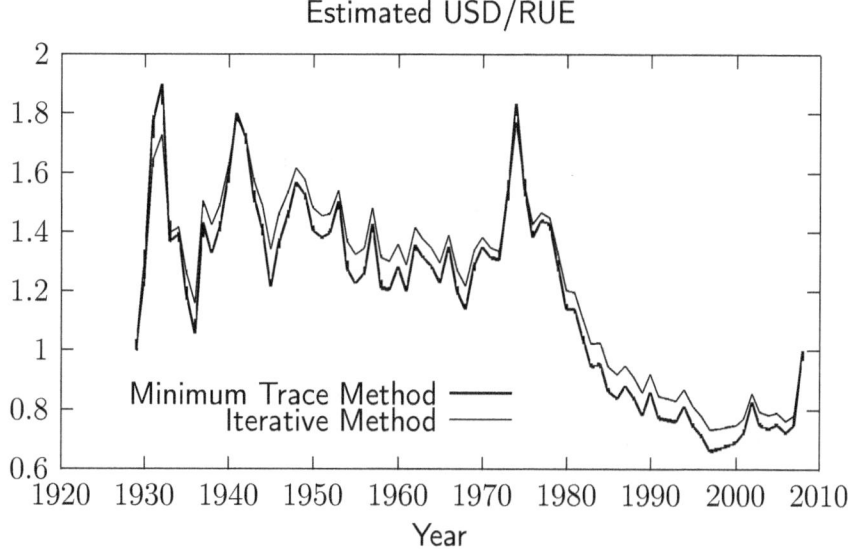

Figure 8.1 USD/RUE estimated from CRSP S&P 500 value and equal weighted indices, and 90 and 30 day Treasury bill indices.

---

[3]These assets have dividends reinvested, so we can assume zero Net Income Yields.

the return of the minimum variance portfolio as a linear combination of assets under our estimated RUE numeraire.

Using the Minimum Trace Method we calculate a RUE denominated Sharpe ratio of 0.2 for the S&P 500 with dividends reinvested. The volatility of consumption per capita denominated in RUE is 9.5% which suggests $\gamma \geq 2.5$ which is within the range expected.

Using the Iterative Method we calculate a RUE denominated Sharpe ratio of 0.2 for the S&P 500 with dividends reinvested. The volatility of consumption per capita denominated in RUE is 11.7% which suggests $\gamma \geq 1.3$ which is also within the range expected, and is a significant improvement on the US dollar denominated analysis.

The Sharpe ratio of the S&P 500 denominated in RUE tends to be lower than the Sharpe ratio denominated in US dollars. This is due to our estimate of the RUE denominated risk-free rate being higher than the US dollar denominated return on 30-day Treasury bills. Assets with small US dollar denominated volatility, such as Treasury bills, have high positive correlation with USD/RUE. Denominated in RUE they then have volatility similar to that of USD/RUE, so do not automatically receive preferential weightings in the RUE denominated minimum variance portfolio used to estimate the composition of the risk-free asset.

We also estimate that consumption per capita is highly positively correlated with USD/RUE with an estimated correlation coefficient of +82.4% using the Minimum Trace Method, and +88.7% using the Iterative Method. This reduces our lower bound for risk-aversion versus the US dollar denominated analysis and also suggests that US dollars are an approximation to a numeraire under which consumption-based asset pricing fails unless log-utility holds.

This estimated correlation stems from the empirical fact that consumption denominated in US dollars has been stable, with lower volatility than that exhibited by USD/RUE. Even without going through the USD/RUE estimation procedure, this result is plausible in light of the contrast between the small volatility of consumption per capita denominated in US dollars, and the relatively large volatility of other assets denominated in US dollars.

We hypothesise that this correlation is a natural result of widespread pegging of income and expenditure in RUE to USD/RUE in the United States. For example, US salaries are commonly specified in advance in US dollars and so average salaries do not vary a great deal denominated in the US dollar asset. Similarly, budgets of US companies and the US government are widely denominated and fixed in US dollars over various periods, pegging US consumption in RUE to USD/RUE.

To conclude, we find no risk premium puzzle under the RUE numeraire. This is an encouraging improvement on the US dollar denominated analysis and suggests that consumption-based asset pricing models are worthy of further research under the RUE numeraire.

— 9 —

Conclusion

Existing theory makes adjustments for inflation as a drift in purchasing power over extended time periods. However, cursory examination of foreign exchange rates tells us that the relative purchasing power of different fiat currencies is volatile on a daily basis, and so it may be reasonable to expect inflation to be a volatile process that exhibits risk (as well as drift) over all time periods.

In this book we presented a new approach that parametrises ratios of exchange between assets by assigning each asset a price process denominated in units we call the 'Ratio Unit of Exchange', or RUE for short. The RUE framework arises from the three core principles of (i) no arbitrage, (ii) equal treatment of all assets, and (iii) recognition of base currencies as assets.

Intuitively, it can be helpful to think of RUE as a unit of value that defines constant purchasing power, although this is entirely optional. The point of RUE is that its symmetrical construction corrects for the preferential treatment of base currency assets under base currency denominated theory, and allows base currencies to exhibit volatile inflation if warranted by empirical evidence. Prices denominated in a fiat base currency can then be seen to be a perspective coloured by the asymmetrical and arbitrary choice of a particular base currency asset.

The usual approach of denominating prices in an arbitrarily chosen base currency asset does not generally attribute risk fairly between assets. In particular, no risk is attributed to the base currency asset. The RUE framework is a way of working under a generalised base currency asset that coincides with the usual base currency approach if and only if our base currency asset has constant price of one denominated in RUE. Another way of thinking about this is that rather than an arbitrarily selected base currency asset being assumed risk-free, the composition of the risk-free asset is left general and open to later estimation.

Perspectives on risk are dependent on the choice of base currency that defines the risk-free asset. For a consistent definition of relative risk we require a non-arbitrary base currency asset corresponding to a unique risk-free asset paying out a spot yield equal to the unique risk-free rate. The RUE framework allows us to work under this non-arbitrary numeraire without needing to identify the composition of the risk-free asset in advance.

An orthogonal basis of investable assets with geometric Brownian dynamics was introduced denominated in RUE, and this basis includes the risk-free asset. The basis can be thought of as the result of a principal components analysis decomposition applied to the returns of RUE denominated real-world composite assets. The basis is assumed to span all possible investable assets.

The value of any asset denominated in its own value is identically one. This means that a US dollar cash account earns zero spot rate due to movements in the RUE price of US dollars, and so relies on wealth to flow into the account if spot rates are to be positive as empirically observed. A 'Net Income Yield' mechanism was introduced to allow for transfers of wealth that result in non-zero spot and forward yields.

Consistent with the principle of equal treatment of all assets, every basis asset is associated with a corresponding Net Income Yield process that results in a transfer of wealth to holders of that basis asset. The Net Income Yield of the Market portfolio was shown to be zero because Net Income Yields are transfers of wealth, and the Market portfolio already holds all assets.

The risk-free rate of return is composed of the RUE price drift and Net Income Yield enjoyed by holders of the risk-free asset. This rate of return was shown to be unique but not necessarily positive. A one RUE risk-free bond paying a Net Income Yield equal to the risk-free rate has zero volatility and drift denominated in RUE due to the uniqueness of the risk-free rate, and so is the base currency asset equivalent to the RUE numeraire.

When viewed from the usual base currency denominated perspective, the RUE framework predicts that the variances of different assets will vary together in response to variation in base currency asset volatility, with higher base currency volatility tending to result in higher asset volatilities. The correlations between base currency denominated asset returns also tend to be higher when base currency volatility is higher and vice-versa. This is consistent with the empirically observed behaviour that volatilities tend to move together, with correlations between asset returns tending to be higher when volatilities are higher and vice-versa.

A consumption-based asset pricing equation, whereby current prices are assumed to be the result of optimal trading strategies maximising expected aggregate utility, was derived denominated in RUE. Instantaneous forward yields were then shown to be the result of expected future Net Income Yields, and so instantaneous spot and forward yields on the Market portfolio are identically zero.

The price of base currency zero coupon bonds was derived and the usual formula for forward foreign exchange rates was obtained. Forward foreign exchange rates were shown to be biased predictors of future spot foreign exchange rates, as empirically observed.

CAPM is a special case of the consumption-based pricing equation and was derived denominated in RUE. This derivation told us that the empirically high correlation between US consumption denominated in RUE and the RUE price of US dollars suggests that US dollar cash may be a better approximation to systematic risk than the Market portfolio. Moreover, we showed that to the extent that this is not true, US dollars will instead appear as illusory systematic risk denominated in US dollars.

A special numeraire under which identity utility holds was introduced, and how utility functions transform under change of numeraire was investigated. Log-utility was shown to be invariant to choice of base currency, so either holds under all numeraires or under none. Consumption-based asset pricing was shown to fail under base currencies perfectly correlated with consumption unless log-utility holds. Given that the RUE price of US dollars is highly correlated with US consumption, US dollars are an approximation to a numeraire under which consumption-based asset pricing fails unless log-utility holds. Furthermore, if log-utility holds, US dollar prices would appear risk-neutral.

Two possible ways to estimate the exchange rate between US dollars and RUE were presented. The Minimum Trace Method involves estimating RUE to minimise the sum of the variances of real-world assets denominated in our estimated RUE numeraire. The Iterative Method is a generalisation of the Minimum Trace Method that relies on robustly estimating the composition of the risk-free asset under RUE. Both of these techniques were employed to estimate RUE empirically.

The US Equity Risk Premium Puzzle was imported into the RUE framework and our empirical estimates of RUE were used to calculate lower bounds for risk aversion. These bounds were in broad agreement with expectations. There are two main effects that reduce this lower bound. Firstly, US dollars are an arbitrarily defined risk-free asset when using US dollars as a base currency. Secondly, high correlation between the US dollar asset and US consumption per capita, denominated in RUE, causes consumption-based asset pricing to fail denominated in US dollars unless log-utility holds. We hypothesise that this correlation is a result of widespread pegging of US income and expenditure to US dollar denominated constants.

To conclude, the RUE framework is a very general approach with wide applicability. It provides a parsimonious solution to the problem of arbitrary base currency choice and generalises existing theory.

Bibliography

[1] T. Andersen, T. Bollerslev, F. Diebold, and H. Ebens. The distribution of realized stock return volatility. *Journal of Financial Economics*, 61:43–76, 2001.

[2] J. H. Cochrane. *Asset Pricing*. Princeton University Press, 2001.

[3] I. Friend and M. Blume. The demand for risky assets. *The American Economic Review*, 65:900–922, 1975.

[4] J. Lintner. The valuation of risk assets and the selection of risky investments in stock portfolios and capital budgets. *Review of Economics and Statistics*, 47:13–37, 1965.

[5] H. M. Markowitz. Portfolio selection. *Journal of Finance*, 7:77–91, 1952.

[6] R. Mehra and E. C. Prescott. The equity premium: a puzzle. *Journal of Monetary Economy*, 15:145–161, 1985.

[7] J. Mossin. Portfolio selection. *Econometrica*, 34:768–783, 1966.

[8] W. Sharpe. Capital asset prices: A theory of market equilibrium under conditions of risk. *Journal of Finance*, 19:425–442, 1964.

[9] J. Treynor. Toward a theory of market value of risky assets. Unpublished manuscript. A final version was published in 1999, in Asset Pricing and Portfolio Performance: Models, Strategy and Performance Metrics. Robert A. Korajczyk (editor) London: Risk Books, pp. 15-22., 1962.

www.ingramcontent.com/pod-product-compliance
Lightning Source LLC
Chambersburg PA
CBHW051726170526
45167CB00002B/815